RONALD REAGAN

A LIFE IN PHOTOGRAPHS

Created by David Elliot Cohen

Text by Peter Robinson

**Foreword by Newt Gingrich
and Callista Gingrich**

Includes Six Historic Reagan Speeches

STERLING

New York / London
www.sterlingpublishing.com

B
REAGAN

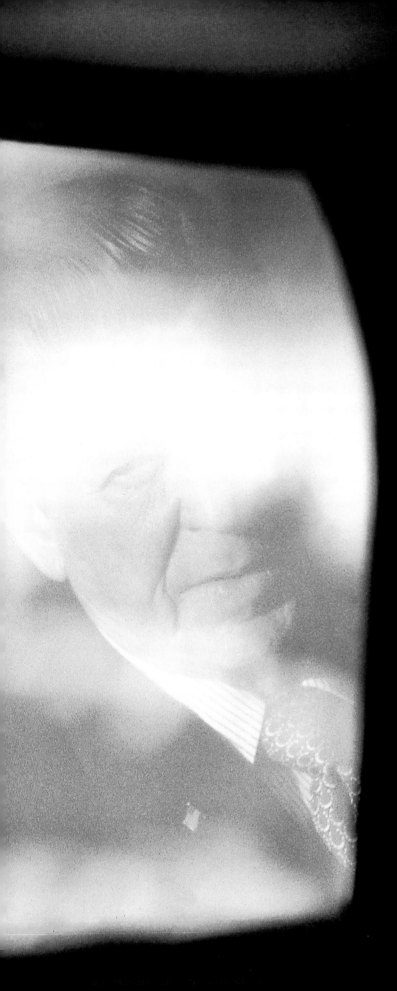

STERLING and the distinctive Sterling logo are registered
trademarks of Sterling Publishing Co., Inc

10 9 8 7 6 5 4 3 2 1

Published by Sterling Publishing Co., Inc
387 Park Avenue South, New York, NY 10016
© 2010 by David Elliot Cohen, Tiburon, CA USA

Distributed in Canada by Sterling Publishing Co.
c/o Canadian Manda Group
165 Dufferin Street
Toronto, Ontario, Canada M6K 3H6

Distributed in the United Kingdom by
GMC Distribution Services
Castle Place, 166 High Street, Lewes
East Sussex, England BN7 1XU

Distributed in Australia by
Capricorn Link (Australia) Pty. Ltd
P.O. Box 704, Windsor, NSW 2756, Australia

Printed in Canada
All rights reserved

Designed by Peter Truskier and David Elliot Cohen
Production by Peter Truskier, Premedia Systems, Inc

Sterling ISBN: 978-1-4027-8057-8
978-1-4027-8237-4 (leatherbound)

FOR INFORMATION about custom editions, special sales
and premium and corporate purchases, please contact the
Sterling Special Sales Department at 800-805-5489 o
specialsales@sterlingpublishing.com

YOUR COMMENTS WELCOME
editor.whatmatters@gmail.com

In memory of Michael Evans (1944–2005), photojournalist
President Reagan's White House photographer, and my friend
—DEC

◀ **THE FUTURE 40TH PRESIDENT OF THE UNITED STATES.**
Candidate Reagan campaigns in New Hampshire in February
1976. Reagan would lose the Republican nomination to incumbent Gerald Ford later that spring. Ford, in turn, would lose to
Democrat Jimmy Carter. But four years later, Reagan would win
both the nomination and the general election. If Reagan was
the most genial of men, he was also the most consistently determined. This is the face that stared down the Evil Empire.

Photograph by David Burnett

FOREWORD

By Newt Gingrich and Callista Gingrich

When we began filming our documentary *Ronald Reagan: Rendezvous with Destiny* in 2008, it became increasingly evident that we were capturing the life of a man whose accomplishments stretched far beyond the eight years he served as president of the United States.

Reagan's legendary quotes—peace through strength, trust but verify, and perhaps most well known, Mr. Gorbachev, tear down this wall—become ever more vivid as you grow to understand the colorful life that so strongly forged his character and his beliefs.

No less than three decades have passed since Ronald Reagan was first elected to the White House in 1980. As president, he ended the Cold War, created unprecedented economic growth, and revived the American spirit. Yet Reagan was no career politician. As you'll discover through these photographs, he was a man of many careers. In fact, he would later call himself a "citizen politician" who entered politics only at the age of 54, when he warned that government was gaining too much power.

Long before that, Ronald Reagan's journey as a young boy in Dixon, Illinois, to his career as a movie star in Hollywood exemplified a purely American story

◀ **RADIO STAR, 1934:** After graduating from Eureka College two years earlier, Reagan tried to find work at one Midwestern radio station after another. At WOC in Davenport, Iowa, he finally got a break. The station manager told Reagan to audition by describing an imaginary football game. "I looked at the microphone," Reagan would later write, "and improvised... *Here we are in the fourth quarter with Western State University leading Eureka College six to nothing. Long blue shadows are settling over the field and a chill wind is blowing in through the end of the stadium.*" For five bucks and bus fare, Reagan was hired to broadcast the Iowa-Minnesota game that weekend. "I'd achieved my dream. I was a sports announcer." Reagan remained in radio, first at WOC, then at WHO in Des Moines, for nearly five years, becoming a celebrity throughout much of the Midwest.

founded on enthusiasm and hard work. Whether he was a lifeguard, student, collegiate athlete, movie star, or president, Reagan was committed to a belief in the promise of America.

One of the most influential periods in Reagan's life was the eight years he spent not as president but as a spokesman for General Electric. In 1952, when his movie career was coming to a close, Reagan accepted a traveling position with GE to promote the company's innovations. He hosted GE's Saturday night television show and toured the country, speaking with thousands of hardworking Americans at GE plants across the nation. His speeches, which he wrote himself, focused on the benefits of the free market system and the inefficiency of big government. He gained invaluable experience giving speeches and articulating the lessons he learned about the proper role of government in free enterprise from the perspective of American workers.

> Whether he was a lifeguard, student, collegiate athlete, movie star, or president, Ronald Reagan was committed to a belief in the promise of America.

Just 12 years after he joined General Electric, Reagan's breakthrough as a great communicator came in 1964 when he gave a televised address on behalf of Republican candidate Barry Goldwater—now simply known as "the speech." At a time when the mood in America and the Republican Party was grim, Reagan offered an inspiring message of hope, optimism, and opportunity.

After he served as governor of California, Reagan's bid for the Republican nomination in 1976 was met with defeat when he narrowly lost to incumbent president Gerald Ford. Yet even after suffering a heartbreaking loss that evening, Reagan once again proved himself a leader. Rather than give a typical concession speech, he shared a message of unity and victory for America.

It is telling that even after suffering such a disappointing loss, Reagan—who was nearly 70 years old by 1980—resolved to try again.

In many of our historical fiction novels, we explore "what if" scenarios and contemplate how the course of history would have changed if just one event had taken place differently. You might ask yourself, What if Ronald Reagan had not run for president in 1980? What if he had decided he was too old, too tired, and instead decided to retire happily to his ranch in California?

It takes a man of remarkable courage and conviction to do what Reagan did in his run for the presidency in 1980. He pledged to the American people his every effort to help our nation keep its "rendezvous with destiny." His belief in the American people and his vision of freedom and prosperity for our nation offered hope at the same time President Jimmy Carter was lamenting America's "crisis of confidence."

Upon his inauguration as the 40th president of the United States of America, many still underestimated Reagan's ability. His charm and optimistic nature, displayed so clearly throughout these photographs, were often mistaken for weakness. Yet Reagan knew what he believed and proved to be a man of great strength and conviction.

After being shot during an assassination attempt just 70 days into his presidency, Reagan believed that he had been spared for a purpose and resolved to dedicate his life to God. Thus, his commitment to freedom and to the American people was strengthened.

The powerful lessons that Ronald Reagan learned throughout his life, as expressed through this lively photographic collection, contributed to his success in delegitimizing the Soviet Union and ending the Cold War. As president of the Screen Actors Guild, he learned to negotiate; as spokesman for GE, he learned to communicate effectively with everyday Americans; and as governor of California, he learned how to work with a Democratic legislature. His frank language challenging Gorbachev to tear down the Berlin Wall clearly communicated to the world America's moral authority in the Cold War (despite many attempts by the U.S. State Department to remove the phrase).

When the Berlin Wall came down in November 1989, Reagan had just finished his second term as president. Although historians may argue about who was most responsible for the end of the Cold War, President Reagan's prediction that the Soviet Union was destined for the ash-heap of history came true. It came true not only because Reagan believed it was possible, but also because he helped America believe it was possible.

We believe the remarkable life of Ronald Reagan will continue to inspire Americans for generations to come. Through this photographic collection, you will embark upon the lifelong journey of a man who made a profound impact on our nation and the world.

▲ **THE REAGAN BOYS:** Neil, born in 1908, and Ronald, born in 1911, in a photograph taken in 1912. Ronald would look after his big brother throughout his young adulthood, persuading Neil to quit work to attend Eureka College, then finding jobs for him in radio and, later, in Hollywood. Neil, who became a Republican in the early 1930s, some three decades earlier than his little brother, would return the favor by persuading Ronald to make campaign appearances on behalf of Republican presidential candidate Barry Goldwater in 1964. Those appearances launched Ronald Reagan into politics.

▶ **FAMILY PORTRAIT, CIRCA 1916:** Parents Jack and Nelle Reagan with sons "Moon" and "Dutch." Neil acquired his nickname from Moon Mullins, a popular comic strip character. Ronald was dubbed "Dutch" because his chubby cheeks and pageboy haircut reminded his father of "a fat little Dutchman." Although the photograph's pose is idyllic, the family suffered its share of heartbreak. Jack, a shoe salesman and store manager, was an alcoholic who had trouble holding a job, moving the family from one Illinois town to another.

▲ **FOURTH GRADE CLASS IN 1920:** Reagan appears in the second row, far left, his hand on his chin. Although outgoing all his life, Reagan formed few close friendships, perhaps because his father moved the family often. This photograph was taken in Tampico, one of a number of Illinois towns in which the family lived before settling in Dixon. Although former defense secretary Clark Clifford would decades later deride Reagan as an "amiable dunce," the evidence suggests otherwise. Able to read at five, Reagan received good grades in school, pored over books and newspapers, and wrote imaginative stories.

◀ **"DUTCH" REAGAN OF DIXON, ILLINOIS:** Shoulders squared, feet firmly planted—an American boy. During Reagan's boyhood, the settling of the prairie and the Civil War both remained living memories—Civil War veterans still marched each year in Armistice Day parades—placing Reagan in direct contact with mythic aspects of American history. "Dutch" also experienced the simple goodness of early 20th-century prairie life. Despite his father's alcoholism, Reagan would later write, he remembered his boyhood as "one of those rare Huck Finn–Tom Sawyer idylls."

▲ **LIFESAVER:** From 1927, the year of this photograph, until 1932, Reagan spent his summers as a lifeguard at Lowell Park, just north of Dixon, Illinois, where a stretch of the Rock River had been designated for swimming. The river currents proved tricky, and during these six summers Reagan saved no fewer than 77 swimmers from drowning, a number of which he was always proud—and that historians would confirm.

◄ **CAPTAIN OF THE SWIM TEAM:** From 1928 to 1932 Reagan attended Eureka College, a small school about 100 miles south of his hometown of Dixon. Eureka was founded in 1855 by members of his mother's religious denomination, the Disciples of Christ. Majoring in economics, Reagan discovered that his memory was so good—nearly photographic—that he could earn acceptable grades by cramming before exams. "My principal academic ambition at Eureka," Reagan would later write, "was to maintain the C average I needed to remain eligible for football, swimming, track, and the other school activities I participated in."

▲ **EUREKA COLLEGE FOOTBALL:** Ronald Reagan, first row, fourth from the right, played for the Red Devils from 1928 to 1932. When Reagan told Ralph "Mac" McKinzie, the football coach, that he couldn't afford to return to Eureka for his sophomore year, McKinzie arranged for the college to give Reagan a Needy Student Scholarship, covering half his tuition, and to defer the remainder until after Reagan graduated. McKinzie also arranged for Reagan to earn extra money washing dishes in the girls' dormitory. "It wasn't the worst job I've ever had," Reagan would often quip.

▶ **THE GUARD, 1929:** Ronald Reagan, lean, handsome, self-confident. But the Depression had just begun, and the shoe store at which his father worked soon failed. This forced his father, Jack, to accept a position at another shoe store on the outskirts of Springfield, some 200 miles from Dixon and his wife. "During the football season," Reagan later wrote, "our team stayed overnight in Springfield, and Moon and I talked Mac into letting us leave the hotel for a few hours... We found Jack in a run-down neighborhood... His store was a grim, tiny hole-in-the-wall... My eyes filled and I looked away, not wanting him to see the tears."

At twenty-two
I'd achieved my
dream: I was a
sports announcer.
If I had stopped
there, I believe I
would have been
happy the rest of
my life.

—*An American Life*, 1990

▶ **AT THE MICROPHONE:** "Dutch" Reagan worked at WHO in Des Moines, Iowa, from 1934 to 1937, honing the conversational delivery that would become his hallmark. His specialty at WHO: describing Chicago Cubs baseball games from the simple, play-by-play accounts he received by telegraph. This required him to invent the color and details. During one game, as Reagan later loved to recount, the telegraph broke down. Reagan kept the broadcast going by having the batter foul off pitches until the machine was repaired.

▲ **MOVIE STAR:** Reagan in Hollywood with his parents, 1937 or 1938. When his radio station, WHO, assigned Reagan to report on the Chicago Cubs during their 1937 spring training on Catalina Island, just off the California coast, Reagan stopped in Los Angeles, where he looked up a minor actress he had known in radio. The actress introduced him to an agent, the agent arranged for him to take a screen test, and on the basis of that single screen test Warner Brothers offered him a contract. Reagan moved his parents to Los Angeles a few months later.

▶ **REGIONAL CELEBRITY:** Ronald Reagan visiting East High School in Des Moines, Iowa, 1936. Reagan launched his speaking career while he was still in his 20s, giving inspirational talks to students, youth groups, and civics organizations. By the time he became president, the "Great Communicator," as the press began calling him, had spent almost half a century developing his skills as a public speaker.

▲ **MIDWESTERNERS IN HOLLYWOOD:** A publicity shot for the Warner Brothers film *Brother Rat*. Ronald Reagan of Dixon, Illinois, and Jane Wyman of St. Joseph, Missouri, met during the filming of this, Reagan's ninth movie. In 1939, powerful Hollywood gossip columnist Louella Parsons, also of little Dixon, Illinois, invited Reagan and Wyman to join a nine-week "stars of tomorrow" tour. Romance blossomed.

▶ **STARS AND NEWLYWEDS:** Ronald Reagan, 28, and Jane Wyman, 23, at their wedding reception, at the home of Louella Parsons, on January 25, 1940. The marriage was Reagan's first. It appears to have been Wyman's third. Awaiting divorce from apparel manufacturer Myron Futterman when she met Reagan—the divorce was finalized in December 1938—she had been married still earlier to salesman Ernest Wyman. After divorcing Reagan in 1948, she married and divorced Hollywood bandleader and composer Fred Karger—twice.

▲ **THE GIPPER:** Ronald Reagan as George Gipp, the legendary Notre Dame football player in the 1940 film *Knute Rockne, All American.* The producer initially turned Reagan down for the role because he didn't look like a football player. So Reagan drove home, rifled through the trunk he had brought with him from Iowa, found a picture in which he appeared in his Eureka football uniform, and drove back to the producer's office. Reagan got the role—and a new nickname.

◀ **BLUE SKIES:** A publicity photograph from the 1940s. It is easy enough to imagine why Reagan is beaming. He was now an established star, a homeowner, and a husband and father able to provide for his family on a scale that even the wealthiest citizens back in Dixon, Illinois, would have been unable to match.

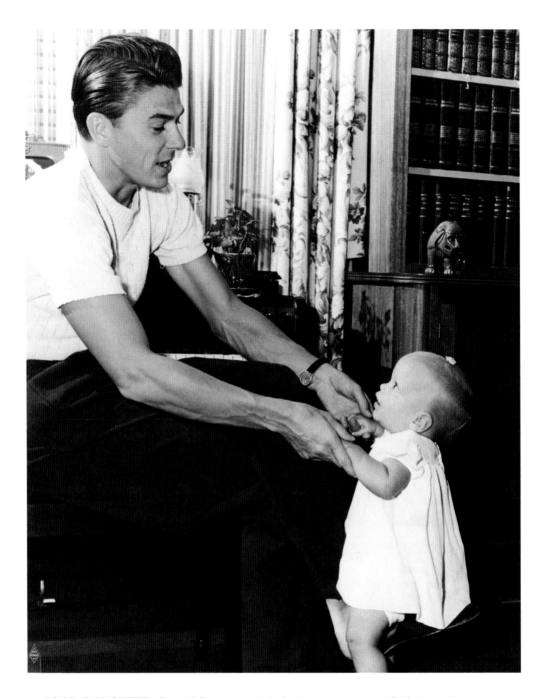

▲ **GOOD DAUGHTER:** Ronald Reagan with baby Maureen, circa 1942. Jane Wyman gave birth to Maureen in 1941, the year after she married Reagan. Four years later, in 1945, the couple adopted Michael, and in 1947, a second daughter, Christine, died soon after her birth. Reagan would always remain particularly close to Maureen, or, as he called her, "Mermie." Maureen, in turn, would embrace her father's politics, serve on the board of her father's alma mater and become a spokesperson for the Alzheimer's Association after her father was stricken with the disease.

▲ **MOTHER NELLE:** She imparted to her son a simple, straightforward Christian faith, an unabashed patriotism, and a profound belief in the essential goodness of ordinary people. Reagan wrote that his mother "always expected to find the best in people and often did." After her husband, Jack, died of a heart attack at age 58 in 1941, Nelle remained in Southern California, helping Reagan with his fan mail and volunteering at local hospitals. She died at age 79 in 1962.

I didn't think much of the inefficiency, empire building, and business-as-usual attitude that existed in wartime under the civil service system.

—*An American Life*, 1990

◄ **CAPT. REAGAN:** Since his poor eyesight—Reagan was an early user of contact lenses—rendered him ineligible for combat duty, Reagan served during World War II in the First Motion Picture Unit in Culver City, California. "One of the doctors…told me after checking my eyes," Reagan would later write, "that if they sent me overseas I'd shoot a general. The other doctor said, 'Yes, and you'd miss him.'"

▲ **TESTIFYING:** Reagan answers questions from the House Un-American Activities Committee, 1947. Serving the first of his six one-year terms as president of the Screen Actors Guild, Reagan condemned communism but insisted on adhering to democratic ideals in resisting it. "I detest, I abhor their philosophy," Reagan said. "But at the same time I never as a citizen want to see our country…compromise any of our democratic principles through…fear or resentment. I still think democracy can do it."

◄ **IN A CURTISS P-40 WARHAWK:** A still from the 1943 Army Air Force training film *Identification of a Japanese Zero*, one of the more than 400 training and morale films that Reagan helped to produce. Reagan also helped to recruit technicians, actors, and directors. "Pretty soon," he later wrote, "I was offering majors' insignias to half-million-dollar-a-year movie directors."

From my mother, I
learned the value of
prayer, how to have
dreams and believe
I could make them
come true.

—*An American Life*, 1990

◄ **HOMETOWN BOY MAKES GOOD:** In 1950 Reagan returned to Dixon, Illinois, as a movie star. He and his mother attended a local festival, "Injun Summer Days," received the key
to the city, and found themselves celebrated by one civic group
after another, including the fire department. Note Nelle Reagan's hand on her son's leg, as if to prevent him from falling—a
simple gesture that sums up her lifelong devotion to her son.

◀◀ ENGAGEMENT PHOTO, 1952 (PREVIOUS PAGES): In 1948 Jane Wyman divorced Reagan, perhaps because, having become a major star herself—she received an Academy Award for her role in *Johnny Belinda*—she felt she no longer needed him. Devastated, Reagan entered the darkest period of his life. Then, in 1949, he met Nancy Davis, a contract player with MGM. Davis was constantly confused with another actress of the same name, and she asked if Reagan, in his second term as president of the Screen Actors Guild, could help. A brief meeting turned into a dinner date, then several more. Three years later, over dinner at Chasen's, their favorite Los Angeles restaurant, Reagan proposed. Although she had acted on Broadway and in a number of films, Nancy would later explain, all she ever really wanted was a happy marriage. She was about to get it—and give Reagan the love and stability he craved.

◀◀ WEDDING DAY, MARCH 4, 1952 (PREVIOUS PAGES): After a wedding ceremony at the Little Brown Church in Studio City, California, the Reagans attended a reception at the Toluca Lake home of Reagan's best man, Academy Award winner and major star William Holden, and his wife, actress Brenda Marshall (née Ardis Gaines). "I told you once," Reagan wrote to Nancy on their anniversary 31 years later, "it was like an adolescent's dream of what marriage should be like. That hasn't changed."

▶ THE OUT-OF-TOWNERS: The newlywed Reagans at Manhattan's trendy Stork Club, a midcentury celebrity hangout that gossip columnist Walter Winchell once called "New York's New Yorkiest place."

STORK CLUB

◄ **THE IN-LAWS:** A rising star before World War II, Reagan found his movie career faltering when the war ended. Here he poses with Nancy, his mother, Nelle, and Nancy's parents, Dr. Loyal and Edith Davis, on the set of the forgettable 1953 Reagan vehicle *Tropic Zone*. As Nancy would later write of this period, she and her husband "couldn't afford to furnish our living room." To augment the family income, she returned to work. "I took a part in a film called *Donovan's Brain*, a science-fiction picture in which Lew Ayres plays a scientist who tries to keep a brain alive and is taken over by it."

◄ **TV HOST:** In 1954 Reagan began hosting *General Electric Theater*, one of the era's most popular television programs. In those days Hollywood looked down its nose at television; Reagan would likely have had nothing to do with *General Electric Theater* if the movie studios hadn't been offering him such second-rate material that he had gone 14 months without accepting a role. But his more than eight years at *General Electric Theater* solved his financial problems and enabled him to master television more completely than any other politician of the 20th century.

▲ **GOODWILL VISIT:** As a General Electric spokesman, Reagan crisscrossed the country, honing his speaking skills and answering questions on the issues of the day from thousands of working people. In time, he began supplementing his inspirational talks with remarks about the importance of free markets and the threat of Soviet communism. Concerned that Reagan was becoming too outspoken, GE dismissed him in 1962. By then he had changed his voter registration to Republican and begun to develop a political following.

I'm convinced that today the majority of Americans want what those first Americans wanted: A better life for themselves and their children.

—NATIONALLY TELEVISED SPEECH, JULY 6, 1976

◄ **CHRISTENING:** Ronald Reagan, Nancy Reagan, infant Ron Reagan, Patricia Reagan, movie star Robert Taylor, his wife, Ursula Taylor, and the Reverend H. Warren Allen at Ron's christening. Reagan began a second family with Nancy in 1952, when she gave birth to Patricia (later "Patti"). After two miscarriages, Nancy gave birth to Ron in 1958.

▲ **HOUSE OF THE FUTURE:** Ronald Reagan, son Ron, Nancy Reagan, and daughter Patricia at their home on San Onofre Drive in Pacific Palisades in 1960. Here, General Electric once again proved a benefactor. In return for permitting the house to be used in advertisements, GE helped the Reagans build a "house of the future," equipping the home with all the latest GE appliances. The home would remain their principal residence until Reagan became president in 1981.

▲ **CORONADO, CALIFORNIA, 1962:** All four of Reagan's children—Maureen and Michael, his children with Jane Wyman, and Patti and Ron, his children with Nancy—recognized that, although Reagan loved them, he remained in some ways distant from them. Because Reagan's own father was an alcoholic, Reagan "didn't really have a role model himself for a father," Ron would later say. "He was a terrific father up until adolescence. But when adolescence hits, it's no longer going out in the backyard and throwing the football around. Instead you want to learn adult stuff and have adult conversations...That's when the relationship started to sort of slip away. An adolescent is an adolescent—a big pain. That made him very uncomfortable." In this picture, father and son—or, as they were to Nancy, Ronnie and Ron.

If ever God gave me evidence that He had a plan for me, it was the night He brought Nancy into my life. I have spent many hours of my life giving speeches and expressing my opinions. But it is almost impossible for me to express fully how deeply I love Nancy and how much she has filled my life. Sometimes, I think my life really began when I met Nancy.

—*An American Life*, 1990

▲ **SUMMER OF '64:** Reagan may have remained at a remove from his children, but he was smitten with Nancy all his life, constantly writing her love letters. Intimate, warm, gentle, and playful, Reagan addressed his wife in these letters as "Nancy Pants," "Nancy Poo," "Muffin," and "Mommie" while signing himself, as governor of California, "Your in Luv Guv," and then, as president, "Prexy." "I more than love you," he would write to her when in the White House. "I'm not whole without you... When you aren't there I'm no place, just lost in time & space."

A TIME FOR CHOOSING

October 27, 1964

Campaigning for Republican presidential candidate Barry Goldwater in 1964, Ronald Reagan delivered "A Time for Choosing" at rallies and at the Republican National Convention in San Francisco. The speech proved so effective that Goldwater supporters bought time on television, enabling Reagan to present it to a national audience. Below, the text of the address as Reagan delivered it in the recorded program that was broadcast on October 27, 1964. "A Time for Choosing" transformed the public perception of Reagan. Before the broadcast, he was an actor who dabbled in politics. After the broadcast, he was a figure of national standing. Although Goldwater would lose the election in a landslide, Reagan would just two years later win election as governor of California, becoming a contender for the presidency itself.

I have spent most of my life as a Democrat. I recently have seen fit to follow another course. I believe that the issues confronting us cross party lines. Now, one side in this campaign has been telling us that the issues of this election are the maintenance of peace and prosperity. The line has been used, "We've never had it so good."

But I have an uncomfortable feeling that this prosperity isn't something on which we can base our hopes for the future. No nation in history has ever survived a tax burden that reached a third of its national income. Today, 37 cents out of every

▶ **TIMELESS VISION:** Speaking on behalf of Republican presidential candidate Barry Goldwater (left) at the International Hotel in Los Angeles, 1964. His many appearances for Goldwater showed Reagan in a new light—a fully formed political figure and a man of commanding presence who knew precisely where he stood.

dollar earned in this country is the tax collector's share,[1] and yet our government continues to spend $17 million a day more than the government takes in. We haven't balanced our budget 28 out of the last 34 years. We've raised our debt limit three times in the last 12 months, and now our national debt is one and a half times bigger than all the combined debts of all the nations of the world. We have $15 billion in gold in our treasury; we don't own an ounce. Foreign dollar claims are $27.3 billion. And we've just had announced that the dollar of 1939 will now purchase 45 cents in its total value.

No nation in history has ever survived a tax burden that reached a third of its national income.

As for the peace that we would preserve, I wonder who among us would like to approach the wife or mother whose husband or son has died in South Vietnam and ask them if they think this is a peace that should be maintained indefinitely. Do they mean peace, or do they mean we just want to be left in peace? There can be no real peace while one American is dying someplace in the world for the rest of us. We're at war with the most dangerous enemy that has ever faced mankind in his long climb from the swamp to the stars, and it's been said if we lose that war, and in so doing lose this way of freedom of ours, history will record with the greatest astonishment that those who had the most to lose did the least to prevent its happening. Well, I think it's time we ask ourselves if we still know the freedoms that were intended for us by the Founding Fathers.

Not too long ago, two friends of mine were talking to a Cuban refugee, a businessman who had escaped from Castro, and in the midst of his story one of my friends turned to the other and said, "We don't know how lucky we are." And the Cuban stopped and said, "How lucky you are? I had someplace to escape to." And in that sentence he told us the entire story. If we lose freedom here, there's no place to escape to. This is the last stand on earth.

And this idea that government is beholden to the people, that it has no other source of power except the sovereign people, is still the newest and the most unique idea in all the long history of man's relation to man.

[1] In 1964, at the time of this speech, the top federal marginal tax rate was 77 percent. When Reagan stepped down as president in 1988, the top marginal rate was 28 percent.

This is the issue of this election: whether we believe in our capacity for self-government, or whether we abandon the American revolution and confess that a little intellectual elite in a far-distant capital can plan our lives for us better than we can plan them ourselves.

You and I are told increasingly we have to choose between a left or right. Well, I'd like to suggest there is no such thing as a left or right. There's only an up or down—[up to] man's [age-old] dream, the ultimate in individual freedom consistent with law and order, or down to the ant heap of totalitarianism. And regardless of their sincerity, their humanitarian motives, those who would trade our freedom for security have embarked on this downward course.

In this vote-harvesting time, they use terms like the "Great Society,"[2] or, as we were told a few days ago by the president, we must accept greater government activity in the affairs of the people. But they've been a little more explicit in the past and among themselves; and all of the things I now will quote have appeared in print.

> We're at war with the most dangerous enemy that has ever faced mankind in his long climb from the swamp to the stars...

These are not Republican accusations. For example, they have voices that say, "The Cold War will end through our acceptance of a not undemocratic socialism." Another voice says, "The profit motive has become outmoded. It must be replaced by the incentives of the welfare state." Or "Our traditional system of individual freedom is incapable of solving the complex problems of the 20th century." Senator Fulbright[3] has said at Stanford University that the Constitution is outmoded. He referred to the president as "our moral teacher and our leader," and he says he is "hobbled in his task by the restrictions of power imposed on him by this antiquated document." He must "be freed," so that he "can do for us" what he knows "is

[2] The Great Society was the name applied to a set of domestic programs proposed or enacted on the initiative of President Lyndon B. Johnson (1963-69). Its hallmarks included the War on Poverty and the establishment of Medicare and Medicaid.

[3] J. William Fulbright was a powerful Democratic senator from Arkansas from 1945 to 1974. He served as chairman of the Senate Foreign Relations Committee from 1959 to 1974.

best." And Senator Clark[4] of Pennsylvania, another articulate spokesman, defines liberalism as "meeting the material needs of the masses through the full power of centralized government."

Well, I, for one, resent it when a representative of the people refers to you and me, the free men and women of this country, as "the masses." This is a term we haven't applied to ourselves in America. But beyond that, "the full power of centralized government"—this was the very thing the Founding Fathers sought to minimize. They knew that governments don't control things. A government can't control the economy without controlling people. And they know when a government sets out to do that, it must use force and coercion to achieve its purpose. They also knew, those Founding Fathers, that outside of its legitimate functions, government does nothing as well or as economically as the private sector of the economy.

> The Founding Fathers knew that outside of its legitimate functions, government does nothing as well or as economically as the private sector.

Now, we have no better example of this than government's involvement in the farm economy over the last 30 years. Since 1955, the cost of this program has nearly doubled. One-fourth of farming in America is responsible for 85 percent of the farm surplus. Three-fourths of farming is out on the free market and has known a 21 percent increase in the per capita consumption of all its produce. You see, that one-fourth of farming—that's regulated and controlled by the federal government. In the last three years we've spent $43 in the feed grain program for every dollar bushel of corn we don't grow.

Senator Humphrey[5] last week charged that Barry Goldwater, as president, would seek to eliminate farmers. He should do his homework a little better, because

---

[4] Joseph Clark, former mayor of Philadelphia, was a Democratic senator from 1957 until 1969, when Republican Richard Schweiker defeated him.

[5] Hubert H. Humphrey was a Democratic senator from Minnesota from 1949 until 1964 and again from 1971 until 1978. At the time of this speech, he was Lyndon Johnson's vice-presidential candidate. Johnson and Humphrey defeated Republican Barry Goldwater and his running mate, U.S. Representative William Miller of New York, on November 3, 1964.

he'll find out that we've had a decline of 5 million in the farm population under these government programs. He'll also find that the Democratic administration has sought to get from Congress [an] extension of the farm program to include that three-fourths that is now free. He'll find that they've also asked for the right to imprison farmers who wouldn't keep books as prescribed by the federal government. The secretary of agriculture asked for the right to seize farms through condemnation and resell them to other individuals. And contained in that same program was a provision that would have allowed the federal government to remove 2 million farmers from the soil.

At the same time, there's been an increase in the Department of Agriculture employees. There's now one for every 30 farms in the United States, and still they can't tell us how 66 shiploads of grain headed for Austria disappeared without a trace and Billie Sol Estes[6] never left shore.

Every responsible farmer and farm organization has repeatedly asked the government to free the farm economy, but who are farmers to know what's best for them? The wheat farmers voted against a wheat program. The government passed it anyway. Now the price of bread goes up; the price of wheat to the farmer goes down.

Meanwhile, back in the city, under urban renewal the assault on freedom carries on. Private property rights [are] so diluted that public interest is almost anything a few government planners decide it should be. In a program that takes from the needy and gives to the greedy, we see such spectacles as in Cleveland, Ohio, a million-and-a-half-dollar building completed only three years ago must be destroyed to make way for what government officials call a "more compatible use of the land."

The president tells us he's now going to start building public housing units in the thousands, where heretofore we've only built them in the hundreds. But FHA[7] and the Veterans Administration tell us they have 120,000 housing units they've taken back through mortgage foreclosure. For three decades, we've sought to solve the problems of unemployment through government planning, and the more the plans

---

[6] Billie Sol Estes was a scandal-ridden Texas financier closely associated with Lyndon Johnson during Johnson's time as a senator from Texas. He allegedly made a fortune by defrauding the federal surplus grain program.

[7] The primary function of the Federal Housing Administration, which was created during the Great Depression, is to insure mortgages.

fail, the more the planners plan. The latest is the Area Redevelopment Agency.[8]

They've just declared Rice County, Kansas, a depressed area. Rice County, Kansas, has 200 oil wells, and the 14,000 people there have over $30 million on deposit in personal savings in their banks. And when the government tells you you're depressed, lie down and be depressed.

> We have so many people who can't see a fat man standing beside a thin one without coming to the conclusion the fat man got that way by taking advantage of the thin one.

We have so many people who can't see a fat man standing beside a thin one without coming to the conclusion the fat man got that way by taking advantage of the thin one. So they're going to solve all the problems of human misery through government and government planning. Well, now, if government planning and welfare had the answer—and they've had almost 30 years of it—shouldn't we expect government to read the score to us once in a while? Shouldn't they be telling us about the decline each year in the number of people needing help? The reduction in the need for public housing?

But the reverse is true. Each year the need grows greater; the program grows greater. We were told four years ago that 17 million people went to bed hungry each night. Well, that was probably true. They were all on a diet. But now we're told that 9.3 million families in this country are poverty-stricken on the basis of earning less than $3,000 a year. Welfare spending [is] 10 times greater than it was in the dark depths of the Depression. We're spending $45 billion on welfare. Now, do a little arithmetic, and you'll find that if we divided the $45 billion up equally among those 9 million poor families, we'd be able to give each family $4,600 a year. And this added to their present income should eliminate poverty. Direct aid to the poor, however, is running only about $600 per family. It would seem that someplace there must be some overhead.

---

[8] Probably a reference to the short-lived Area Redevelopment Administration, which was created in 1961 and remained in operation until 1965. The agency's ostensible goal was to help economically distressed communities in rural and undeveloped areas of the country to develop employment opportunities.

So now we declare "war on poverty," or "You, too, can be a Bobby Baker."[9] Now, do they honestly expect us to believe that if we add $1 billion to the 45 billion we're spending, one more program to the 30-odd we have—and remember, this new program doesn't replace any, it just duplicates existing programs—do they believe that poverty is suddenly going to disappear by magic? Well, in all fairness I should explain there is one part of the new program that isn't duplicated. This is the youth feature. We're now going to solve the dropout problem, juvenile delinquency, by reinstituting something like the old CCC[10] camps, and we're going to put our young people in these camps. But again we do some arithmetic, and we find that we're going to spend, each year, just on room and board for each young person we help, $4,700 a year. We can send them to Harvard for 2,700! Course, don't get me wrong. I'm not suggesting Harvard is the answer to juvenile delinquency.

> The trouble with our liberal friends is not that they're ignorant; it's just that that they know so much that isn't so.

But seriously, what are we doing to those we seek to help? Not too long ago, a judge called me here in Los Angeles. He told me of a young woman who'd come before him for a divorce. She had six children, was pregnant with her seventh. Under his questioning, she revealed her husband was a laborer earning $250 a month. She wanted a divorce to get an $80-dollar raise. She's eligible for $330 a month in the Aid to Dependent Children program. She got the idea from two women in her neighborhood who'd already done that very thing.

Yet any time you and I question the schemes of the do-gooders, we're denounced as being against their humanitarian goals. They say we're always "against" things— we're never "for" anything.

Well, the trouble with our liberal friends is not that they're ignorant; it's just that they know so much that isn't so.

Now, we're for a provision that destitution should not follow unemployment by

---

[9] Bobby Baker was a Washington insider, power broker and political advisor to President Lyndon Johnson. He resigned as secretary for the majority of the U.S. Senate in 1963 amid allegations of corruption and conflict of interest.

[10] The Civilian Conservation Corps (1933–42) was a Depression-era relief program for unemployed men. It provided vocational training through public work related to conservation and the development of natural resources.

reason of old age, and to that end we've accepted Social Security as a step toward meeting the problem.

But we're against those entrusted with this program when they practice deception regarding its fiscal shortcomings, when they charge that any criticism of the program means that we want to end payments to those people who depend on them for a livelihood. They've called it "insurance" to us in a hundred million pieces of literature. But then they appeared before the Supreme Court and they testified it was a welfare program. They only use the term "insurance" to sell it to the people. And they said Social Security dues are a tax for the general use of the government, and the government has used that tax. There is no fund, because Robert Byers, the actuarial head [of the Social Security Administration], appeared before a congressional committee and admitted that Social Security as of this moment is $298 billion in the hole. But he said there should be no cause for worry because as long as they have the power to tax, they could always take away from the people whatever they needed to bail them out of trouble. And they're doing just that.

> No government ever voluntarily reduces itself in size. So governments' programs, once launched, never disappear. Actually, a government bureau is the nearest thing to eternal life we'll ever see on this earth.

A young man, 21 years of age, working at an average salary—his Social Security contribution would, in the open market, buy him an insurance policy that would guarantee $220 a month at age 65. The government promises 127. He could live it up until he's 31 and then take out a policy that would pay more than Social Security. Now, are we so lacking in business sense that we can't put this program on a sound basis, so that people who do require those payments will find they can get them when they're due, that the cupboard isn't bare? Barry Goldwater thinks we can.

At the same time, can't we introduce voluntary features that would permit a citizen who can do better on his own to be excused upon presentation of evidence that he had made provision for the non-earning years? Should we not allow a widow with children to work, and not lose the benefits supposedly paid for by her deceased husband? Shouldn't you and I be allowed to declare who our beneficiaries will be under this program, which we cannot do? I think we're for telling our senior citizens that no one in this country should be denied medical care because of a lack of funds. But I think we're against forcing all citizens, regardless of need, into a compulsory government program, especially when we have such examples, as was announced last week, when France admitted that their Medicare program is now bankrupt. They've come to the end of the road.

In addition, was Barry Goldwater so irresponsible when he suggested that our government give up its program of deliberate, planned inflation, so that when you do get your Social Security pension, a dollar will buy a dollar's worth, and not 45 cents' worth?

I think we're for an international organization where the nations of the world can seek peace. But I think we're against subordinating American interests to an organization that has become so structurally unsound that today you can muster a two-thirds vote on the floor of the General Assembly among nations that represent less than 10 percent of the world's population. I think we're against the hypocrisy of assailing our allies because here and there they cling to a colony, while we engage in a conspiracy of silence and never open our mouths about the millions of people enslaved in the Soviet colonies in the satellite nations.

I think we're for aiding our allies by sharing our material blessings with those nations which share in our fundamental beliefs, but we're against doling out money government-to-government, creating bureaucracy, if not socialism, all over the world. We set out to help 19 countries. We're helping 107. We've spent $146 billion. With that money, we bought a $2-million yacht for Haile Selassie.[11] We bought dress suits for Greek undertakers; extra wives for Kenya government officials. We bought a thousand TV sets for a place where they have no electricity. In the last six years, 52 nations have bought $7 billion worth of our gold, and all 52 are receiving foreign aid from this country.

No government ever voluntarily reduces itself in size. So governments' programs,

[11] Haile Selassie I (b. Tafari Makonnen, 1892–1975) was emperor of Ethiopia from 1930 to 1974.

once launched, never disappear. Actually, a government bureau is the nearest thing to eternal life we'll ever see on this earth.

Federal employees number two and a half million; and federal, state, and local, one out of six of the nation's workforce [is] employed by government. These proliferating bureaus with their thousands of regulations have cost us many of our constitutional safeguards. How many of us realize that today federal agents can invade a man's property without a warrant? They can impose a fine without a formal hearing, let alone a trial by jury. And they can seize and sell his property at auction to enforce the payment of that fine. In Chico County, Arkansas, James Wier overplanted his rice allotment. The government obtained a 17,000-dollar judgment. And a U.S. marshal sold his 960-acre farm at auction. The government said it was necessary as a warning to others to make the system work.

Last February 19 at the University of Minnesota, Norman Thomas, six times candidate for president on the Socialist Party ticket, said, "If Barry Goldwater became president, he would stop the advance of socialism in the United States." I think that's exactly what he will do.

But as a former Democrat, I can tell you Norman Thomas isn't the only man who has drawn this parallel to socialism with the present administration, because back in 1936, Mr. Democrat himself, Al Smith, the great American, came before the American people and charged that the leadership of his party was taking the party of Jefferson, Jackson, and Cleveland down the road under the banners of Marx, Lenin, and Stalin. And he walked away from his party, and he never returned until the day he died—because to this day, the leadership of that party has been taking that party, that honorable party, down the road in the image of the Labour socialist party of England.

Now, it doesn't require expropriation or confiscation of private property or business to impose socialism on a people. What does it mean whether you hold the deed to the—or the title to your business or property if the government holds the power of life and death over that business or property? And such machinery already exists. The government can find some charge to bring against any concern it chooses to prosecute. Every businessman has his own tale of harassment. Somewhere a perversion has taken place. Our natural, unalienable rights are now considered to be a dispensation of government, and freedom has never been so fragile, so close to slipping from our grasp as it is at this moment.

Our Democratic opponents seem unwilling to debate these issues. They want to make you and I believe that this is a contest between two men—that we're to choose just between two personalities. Well, what of this man[12] that they would destroy—and, in destroying, they would destroy that which he represents, the ideas that you and I hold dear? Is he the brash and shallow and trigger-happy man they say he is? Well, I've been privileged to know him "when." I knew him long before he ever dreamed of trying for high office, and I can tell you personally I've never known a man in my life I believed so incapable of doing a dishonest or dishonorable thing.

Our natural, unalienable rights are now considered a dispensation of government, and freedom has never been so fragile, so close to slipping from our grasp as it is at this moment.

This is a man who, in his own business before he entered politics, instituted a profit-sharing plan before unions had ever thought of it. He put in health and medical insurance for all his employees. He took 50 percent of the profits before taxes and set up a retirement program, a pension plan for all his employees. He sent monthly checks for life to an employee who was ill and couldn't work. He provides nursing care for the children of mothers who work in the stores.[13] When Mexico was ravaged by the floods in the Rio Grande, he climbed in his airplane and flew medicine and supplies down there.

An ex-GI told me how he met [Goldwater]. It was the week before Christmas during the Korean War, and he was at the Los Angeles airport trying to get a ride home to Arizona for Christmas. And he said that [there were] a lot of servicemen there and no seats available on the planes. And then a voice came over the loudspeaker and said, "Any men in uniform wanting a ride to Arizona, go to Runway Such-and-such," and they went down there, and there was a fellow named Barry Goldwater sitting in his plane. Every day in those weeks before Christmas, all day long, he'd load up the plane, fly it to Arizona, fly them to their homes, fly back over to get another load.

[12] Republican presidential candidate Barry Goldwater.

[13] Goldwater's, a department store chain based in Phoenix, Arizona, founded by the candidate's grandfather.

During the hectic split-second timing of a campaign, this is a man who took time out to sit beside an old friend who was dying of cancer. His campaign managers were understandably impatient, but he said, "There aren't many left who care what happens to her. I'd like her to know I care." This is a man who said to his 19-year-old son, "There is no foundation like the rock of honesty and fairness, and when you begin to build your life on that rock, with the cement of the faith in God that you have, then you have a real start." This is not a man who could carelessly send other people's sons to war. And that is the issue of this campaign that makes all the other problems I've discussed academic, unless we realize we're in a war that must be won.

You and I have a rendezvous with destiny.

Those who would trade our freedom for the soup kitchen of the welfare state have told us they have a utopian solution of peace without victory. They call their policy "accommodation." And they say if we'll only avoid any direct confrontation with the enemy, he'll forget his evil ways and learn to love us. All who oppose them are indicted as warmongers. They say we offer simple answers to complex problems. Well, perhaps there is a simple answer—not an easy answer, but simple—if you and I have the courage to tell our elected officials that we want our national policy based on what we know in our hearts is morally right.

We cannot buy our security, our freedom from the threat of the bomb, by committing an immorality so great as saying to a billion human beings now enslaved behind the Iron Curtain, "Give up your dreams of freedom because to save our own skins, we're willing to make a deal with your slave masters." Alexander Hamilton said, "A nation which can prefer disgrace to danger is prepared for a master, and deserves one." Now, let's set the record straight. There's no argument over the choice between peace and war, but there's only one guaranteed way you can have peace—and you can have it in the next second—surrender.

Admittedly, there's a risk in any course we follow other than this, but every lesson of history tells us that the greater risk lies in appeasement, and this is the specter our well-meaning liberal friends refuse to face—that their policy of accommodation is appeasement, and it gives no choice between peace and war, only between fight or surrender. If we continue to accommodate, continue to back [up] and retreat, eventually we have to face the final demand—the ultimatum. And what then? When Nikita Khrushchev has told his people he knows what our answer will be. He has told them that we're retreating under the pressure of the Cold War, and someday, when the time comes to deliver the final ultimatum, our surrender will be voluntary, because by that time we will have been weakened from within spiritually, morally, and economically. He believes this because from our side he's heard voices pleading for "peace at any price" or "better Red than dead" or, as one commentator put it, he'd rather "live on his knees than die on his feet."

And therein lies the road to war, because those voices don't speak for the rest of us.

You and I know and do not believe that life is so dear and peace so sweet as to be purchased at the price of chains and slavery. If nothing in life is worth dying for, when did this begin—just in the face of this enemy? Or should Moses have told the children of Israel to live in slavery under the pharaohs? Should Christ have refused the cross? Should the patriots at Concord Bridge have thrown down their guns and refused to fire the "shot heard 'round the world"? The martyrs of history were not fools, and our honored dead who gave their lives to stop the advance of the Nazis didn't die in vain. Where, then, is the road to peace? Well, it's a simple answer, after all.

> We'll preserve for our children this, the last best hope of man on earth, or we'll sentence them to take the last step into a thousand years of darkness.

You and I have the courage to say to our enemies, "There is a price we will not pay." There is a point beyond which they must not advance. And this—this is the meaning in the phrase of Barry Goldwater's "peace through strength." Winston Churchill said, "The destiny of man is not measured by material computations. When great forces are on the move in the world, we learn we're spirits, not animals." And he said, "There's something going on in time and space, and beyond time and space, which, whether we like it or not, spells duty."

You and I have a rendezvous with destiny.

We'll preserve for our children this, the last best hope of man on earth, or we'll sentence them to take the last step into a thousand years of darkness.

We will keep in mind and remember that Barry Goldwater has faith in us. He has faith that you and I have the ability and the dignity and the right to make our own decisions and determine our own destiny.

◀ **VICTORY:** Governor-elect and Nancy Reagan at the Biltmore Hotel in Los Angeles, on election night 1966. Buoyed by his reception while campaigning for Republican presidential candidate Barry Goldwater in 1964, Reagan ran for governor of California two years later. He promised to limit the growth of state government and, responding to anti-war protests in Berkeley, to restore law and order. Seeking a third term, Reagan's opponent, Edmund G. "Pat" Brown, had long dominated California politics. Brown derided Reagan as a mere actor, once reminding schoolchildren that "an actor shot Lincoln." Reagan won in a landslide, carrying 55 of 58 counties to defeat Brown by nearly a million votes.

▲ **THE GOVERNOR:** The 33rd governor of California takes the oath of office from California State Supreme Court Justice Marshall McComb on January 2, 1967. Required by the state constitution to balance the budget, Reagan froze state hiring and reluctantly raised taxes. When revenues later rose, producing a surplus, the governor knew what to do with the extra money. "Send it back," he said, insisting on rebate checks for taxpayers and a subsequent tax cut. Early in his first year the governor signed a bill liberalizing abortion law, an action he later regretted. By contrast, Reagan never regretted his consistently firm stand against anti–Vietnam War protests or sending the National Guard to quell student unrest at the University of California, Berkeley. Easily reelected in 1970, Reagan served as governor for eight years.

From the start, our marriage was like an adolescent's dream of what a marriage should be.

—*An American Life,* 1990

◀ **LOVE STORY:** When this photograph was taken, in the mid-1970s, Ronald Reagan had already served eight years as governor of California and would soon run for president. He had become, in a word, a politician. Aides sought to push him this way and that, the press reported his every misstep, interest groups made unceasing demands, and ordinary voters stopped him every day to ask if he would give them his autograph or pose with them for a snapshot. Here, in the pool at their home in Pacific Palisades, Reagan relaxes with the one person who wanted nothing except his well-being.

Every promise, every opportunity, is still golden in this land... Her heart is full, her future bright.

—Speech to the Republican National Convention, August 23, 1984

▶ **AT THE RANCH, 1976:** A horse lover all his life, Reagan owned three ranches. The first was in Northridge, California; the second was on property near Malibu Lake, now part of Malibu State Park; and the third was on the ridgeline of the Santa Ynez Mountains, north of Santa Barbara. Reagan named the third ranch Rancho del Cielo, the "ranch of heaven." To the east, the land tumbles down and away, spreading to form the green bowl of the Santa Ynez valley. To the west lies the Pacific, with the Channel Islands in the middle distance. Rancho del Cielo, Reagan remarked, felt like "a cathedral with oak trees for walls." This portrait, by Reagan's longtime personal photographer, Michael Evans, was one of Reagan's—and America's—favorites.

The family has always been the cornerstone of American society. Our families nurture, preserve, and pass on to each succeeding generation the values we share and cherish.

—Presidential Proclamation, November 12, 1982

◀ **FAMILY TIES:** The former governor with his family in 1975 or 1976. After leaving the governor's office in January 1975, Reagan returned, with Nancy, to their home on San Onofre Drive in Pacific Palisades. Now a national figure, Reagan devoted himself to speaking engagements, a twice-weekly syndicated newspaper column, and a five-day-a-week syndicated commentary carried on more than 300 local radio stations. "Dad had a big desk in the master bedroom," son Michael Reagan would later explain, "and he was always at that desk, writing. Not almost always. Always."

▲ **ROAD TO THE WHITE HOUSE:** In 1976 Reagan challenged incumbent president Gerald Ford for the Republican presidential nomination, losing by a narrow margin. When Reagan again sought the Republican nomination in 1980, many believed the candidate, then 69, too old for the job. But Reagan displayed more than enough wit and vigor to prove them wrong. After losing a straw poll in Iowa—he made few appearances in the state—he reorganized his campaign, won the New Hampshire primary, and then dominated the rest of the primary season. In this photograph of a Chicago debate moderated by former CBS news commentator Eric Sevareid, Reagan appears with three fellow Republican candidates: Illinois congressman Philip Crane; Reagan's eventual vice president, George Bush; and Illinois congressman John Anderson, who would run in the general election as an independent. Reagan dominates this photograph as thoroughly as he dominated the contest.

▲ **THE NOMINEE:** Having chosen George H. W. Bush as his running mate, Reagan accepts the presidential nomination of the party of Lincoln. Unemployment and inflation had both reached double digits, and Iran held 52 Americans hostage. "They say the United States has had its day in the sun," Reagan said of President Carter and his supporters, "that our nation has passed its zenith. My fellow citizens, I utterly reject that view... I will not stand by and watch this great country destroy itself under mediocre leadership that drifts from one crisis to the next."

President Reagan was a formidable political campaigner, who provided an inspirational voice to America when our people were searching for a clear message of hope and confidence.

—FORMER PRESIDENT JIMMY CARTER, JUNE 7, 2004

▶ **CAMPAIGN TRAIL:** Columbia, South Carolina, October 10, 1980. The race between Reagan and incumbent president Jimmy Carter remained tight for weeks. Then, on October 28, the candidates met for a widely watched presidential debate. When Carter repeatedly tried to portray him as an extremist, Reagan replied, "There you go again," with an easy, sunny smile. In his closing remarks, Reagan asked voters a simple but devastatingly effective question: "Are you better off now than you were four years ago? If so, I encourage you to vote for my opponent. If not, I urge you to vote for me." Over the following weekend, Reagan opened a lead. On Election Day, he won in a landslide, defeating Carter by nearly 10 percentage points, carrying 44 states to Carter's six. Riding Reagan's coattails, Republicans recaptured control of the Senate for the first time in a quarter century.

FIRST INAUGURAL ADDRESS

January 20, 1981

To a few of us here today this is a solemn and most momentous occasion, and yet in the history of our nation it is a commonplace occurrence. The orderly transfer of authority as called for in the Constitution routinely takes place, as it has for almost two centuries, and few of us stop to think how unique we really are. In the eyes of many in the world, this every-four-year ceremony we accept as normal is nothing less than a miracle.

Mr. President, I want our fellow citizens to know how much you did to carry on this tradition. By your gracious cooperation in the transition process, you have shown a watching world that we are a united people pledged to maintaining a political system which guarantees individual liberty to a greater degree than any other, and I thank you and your people for all your help in maintaining the continuity which is the bulwark of our republic.

The business of our nation goes forward. These United States are confronted with an economic affliction of great proportions. We suffer from the longest and one of the worst sustained inflations in our national history. It distorts our economic decisions, penalizes thrift, and crushes the struggling young and the fixed-income elderly alike. It threatens to shatter the lives of millions of our people.

◄ **I DO SOLEMNLY SWEAR:** His left hand on his mother's Bible, Ronald Wilson Reagan takes the presidential oath of office, administered by Chief Justice Warren Burger, becoming the 40th chief executive of the United States of America.

Idle industries have cast workers into unemployment, human misery, and personal indignity. Those who do work are denied a fair return for their labor by a tax system which penalizes successful achievement and keeps us from maintaining full productivity.

But great as our tax burden is, it has not kept pace with public spending. For decades we have piled deficit upon deficit, mortgaging our future and our children's future for the temporary convenience of the present. To continue this long trend is to guarantee tremendous social, cultural, political, and economic upheavals.

> For decades we have piled deficit upon deficit, mortgaging our future and our children's future.

You and I, as individuals, can, by borrowing, live beyond our means, but for only a limited period of time. Why, then, should we think that collectively, as a nation, we're not bound by that same limitation? We must act today in order to preserve tomorrow. And let there be no misunderstanding: We are going to begin to act, beginning today.

The economic ills we suffer have come upon us over several decades. They will not go away in days, weeks, or months, but they will go away. They will go away because we as Americans have the capacity now, as we've had in the past, to do whatever needs to be done to preserve this last and greatest bastion of freedom.

In this present crisis, government is not the solution to our problem; government is the problem. From time to time we've been tempted to believe that society has become too complex to be managed by self-rule, that government by an elite group is superior to government for, by, and of the people. Well, if no one among us is capable of governing himself, then who among us has the capacity to govern someone else? All of us together, in and out of government, must bear the burden. The solutions we seek must be equitable, with no one group singled out to pay a higher price.

We hear much of special interest groups. Well, our concern must be for a special interest group that has been too long neglected. It knows no sectional boundaries or ethnic and racial divisions, and it crosses political party lines. It is made up of men and women who raise our food, patrol our streets, man our mines and factories, teach our children, keep our homes, and heal us when we're sick—professionals, industrialists, shopkeepers, clerks, cabbies, and truck drivers. They are, in short, "we the people," this breed called Americans.

Well, this administration's objective will be a healthy, vigorous, growing economy that provides equal opportunities for all Americans with no barriers born of bigotry or discrimination. Putting America back to work means putting all Americans back to work. Ending inflation means freeing all Americans from the terror of runaway living costs. All must share in the productive work of this "new beginning," and all must share in the bounty of a revived economy. With the idealism and fair play which are the core of our system and our strength, we can have a strong and prosperous America, at peace with itself and the world.

So, as we begin, let us take inventory. We are a nation that has a government—not the other way around. And this makes us special among the nations of the earth. Our government has no power except that granted it by the people. It is time to check and reverse the growth of government, which shows signs of having grown beyond the consent of the governed.

It is my intention to curb the size and influence of the federal establishment and to demand recognition of the distinction between the powers granted to the federal government and those reserved to the states or to the people. All of us need to be reminded that the federal government did not create the states; the states created the federal government.

Now, so there will be no misunderstanding, it's not my intention to do away with government. It is rather to make it work—work with us, not over us; to stand by our side, not ride on our back. Government can and must provide opportunity, not smother it; foster productivity, not stifle it.

If we look to the answer as to why for so many years we achieved so much, prospered as no other people on earth, it was because here in this land we unleashed the energy and individual genius of man to a greater extent than has ever been done before. Freedom and the dignity of the individual have been more available and assured here than in any other place on earth. The price for this freedom at times has been high, but we have never been unwilling to pay that price.

It is no coincidence that our present troubles parallel and are proportionate to

> Government is not the solution to our problem; government is the problem.

the intervention and intrusion in our lives that result from unnecessary and excessive growth of government. It is time for us to realize that we're too great a nation to limit ourselves to small dreams. We're not, as some would have us believe, doomed to an inevitable decline. I do not believe in a fate that will fall on us no matter what we do. I do believe in a fate that will fall on us if we do nothing. So, with all the creative energy at our command, let us begin an era of national renewal. Let us renew our determination, our courage, and our strength. And let us renew our faith and our hope.

> We are a nation that has a government—not the other way around. And this makes us special among the nations of the earth.

We have every right to dream heroic dreams. Those who say that we're in a time when there are not heroes, they just don't know where to look. You can see heroes every day going in and out of factory gates. Others, a handful in number, produce enough food to feed all of us and then the world beyond. You meet heroes across a counter, and they're on both sides of that counter. There are entrepreneurs with faith in themselves and faith in an idea who create new jobs, new wealth and opportunity. They're individuals and families whose taxes support the government and whose voluntary gifts support church, charity, culture, art, and education. Their patriotism is quiet, but deep. Their values sustain our national life.

Now, I have used the words "they" and "their" in speaking of these heroes. I could say "you" and "your," because I'm addressing the heroes of whom I speak— you, the citizens of this blessed land. Your dreams, your hopes, your goals are going to be the dreams, the hopes, and the goals of this administration, so help me God.

We shall reflect the compassion that is so much a part of your makeup. How can we love our country and not love our countrymen; and, loving them, reach out a hand when they fall, heal them when they're sick, and provide opportunity to make them self-sufficient so they will be equal in fact and not just in theory?

Can we solve the problems confronting us? Well, the answer is an unequivocal and emphatic "yes." To paraphrase Winston Churchill, I did not take the oath I've just taken with the intention of presiding over the dissolution of the world's strongest economy.

In the days ahead I will propose removing the roadblocks that have slowed our economy and reduced productivity. Steps will be taken aimed at restoring the balance between the various levels of government. Progress may be slow, measured in inches and feet, not miles, but we will progress. It is time to reawaken this industrial giant, to get government back within its means, and to lighten our punitive tax burden. And these will be our first priorities, and on these principles there will be no compromise.

On the eve of our struggle for independence a man who might have been one of the greatest among the Founding Fathers, Dr. Joseph Warren, president of the Massachusetts Congress, said to his fellow Americans, "Our country is in danger, but not to be despaired of… On you depend the fortunes of America. You are to decide the important questions upon which rest the happiness and the liberty of millions yet unborn. Act worthy of yourselves."

Well, I believe we, the Americans of today, are ready to act worthy of ourselves, ready to

> I do not believe in a fate that will fall on us no matter what we do. I do believe in a fate that will fall on us if we do nothing.

do what must be done to ensure happiness and liberty for ourselves, our children, and our children's children. And as we renew ourselves here in our own land, we will be seen as having greater strength throughout the world. We will again be the exemplar of freedom and a beacon of hope for those who do not now have freedom.

To those neighbors and allies who share our freedom, we will strengthen our historic ties and assure them of our support and firm commitment. We will match loyalty with loyalty. We will strive for mutually beneficial relations. We will not use our friendship to impose on their sovereignty, for our own sovereignty is not for sale.

As for the enemies of freedom, those who are potential adversaries, they will be reminded that peace is the highest aspiration of the American people. We will negotiate for it, sacrifice for it; we will not surrender for it, now or ever.

Our forbearance should never be misunderstood. Our reluctance for conflict should not be misjudged as a failure of will. When action is required to preserve our national security, we will act. We will maintain sufficient strength to prevail if need be, knowing that if we do so we have the best chance of never having to use that strength.

Above all, we must realize that no arsenal, or no weapon in the arsenals of the world, is so formidable as the will and moral courage of free men and women. It is a weapon our adversaries in today's world do not have. It is a weapon that we as Americans do have. Let that be understood by those who practice terrorism and prey upon their neighbors.

As we renew ourselves, we will again be the exemplar of freedom and a beacon of hope for those who do not now have freedom.

I'm told that tens of thousands of prayer meetings are being held on this day, and for that I'm deeply grateful. We are a nation under God, and I believe God intended for us to be free. It would be fitting and good, I think, if on each Inaugural Day in future years it should be declared a day of prayer.

This is the first time in our history that this ceremony has been held, as you've been told, on this West Front of the Capitol. Standing here, one faces a magnificent vista, opening up on this city's special beauty and history. At the end of this open mall are those shrines to the giants on whose shoulders we stand.

Directly in front of me, the monument to a monumental man, George Washington, father of our country. A man of humility who came to greatness reluctantly. He led America out of revolutionary victory into infant nationhood. Off to one side, the stately memorial to Thomas Jefferson. The Declaration of Independence flames with his eloquence. And then, beyond the Reflecting Pool, the dignified columns of the Lincoln Memorial. Whoever would understand in his heart the meaning of America will find it in the life of Abraham Lincoln.

Beyond those monuments to heroism is the Potomac River and, on the far shore, the sloping hills of Arlington National Cemetery, with its row upon row of simple white markers bearing crosses or Stars of David. They add up to only a tiny fraction of the price that has been paid for our freedom.

Each one of those markers is a monument to the kind of hero I spoke of earlier. Their lives ended in places called Belleau Wood, the Argonne, Omaha Beach, Salerno, and halfway around the world on Guadalcanal, Tarawa, Pork Chop Hill, the Chosin Reservoir, and in a hundred rice paddies and jungles of a place called Vietnam.

Under one such marker lies a young man, Martin Treptow, who left his job in a small-town barbershop in 1917 to go to France with the famed Rainbow Division.[1] There, on the western front, he was killed trying to carry a message between battalions under heavy artillery fire.

We're told that on his body was found a diary. On the flyleaf, under the heading "My Pledge," he had written these words: "America must win this war. Therefore I will work, I will save, I will sacrifice, I will endure, I will fight cheerfully and do my utmost, as if the issue of the whole struggle depended on me alone."

The crisis we are facing today does not require of us the kind of sacrifice that Martin Treptow and so many thousands of others were called upon to make. It does require, however, our best effort and our willingness to believe in ourselves and to believe in our capacity to perform great deeds, to believe that together with God's help we can and will resolve the problems which now confront us.

And after all, why shouldn't we believe that? We are Americans.

God bless you, and thank you.

> We must realize that no weapon in the arsenals of the world is so formidable as the will and moral courage of free men and women.

[1] The 42nd Infantry Division of the U.S. Army, which included Army National Guard units from many states.

Peace is the highest aspiration of the American people. We will negotiate for it, sacrifice for it; we will not surrender for it, now or ever.

▶ **INAUGURATION PRESENT:** His inaugural address complete, the new chief executive acknowledges applause. Minutes later, Iran released the 52 American hostages they had held for 444 days. When the returning hostages landed at an American base in West Germany, former president Jimmy Carter was there to greet them, serving as Reagan's emissary.

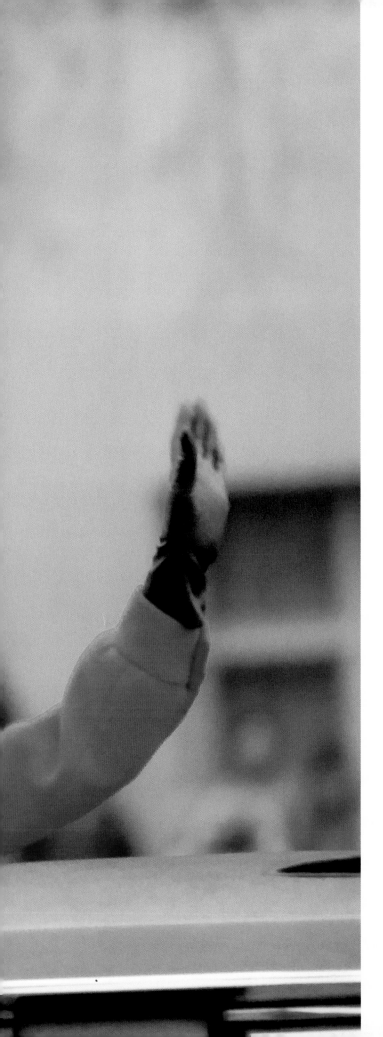

▲ **ELEGANCE REDUX:** The president and Mrs. Reagan pose in the Red Room of the White House before attending a series of nine inaugural balls, January 20, 1981. Reagan's predecessor, Jimmy Carter, took the oath of office in a business suit and attended his inaugural balls in a dinner jacket. Reagan restored a note of formality, taking his oath in a morning coat and attending the balls in white tie and tails. Not that he suppressed his exuberance. Waiting to be announced at one of the balls that night, Reagan looked at himself in a mirror, leapt up, and clicked his heels. "I'm President of the United States of America!" he said, grinning.

◀ **VICTORY LAP:** Riding from the Capitol down Pennsylvania Avenue to the White House, the Reagans wave from their limousine. "I've seen all those photographs that have been printed in various articles of someone slouched looking out the Oval Office windows and then beside it the quote about [the presidency being] the loneliest [job] and so forth," Reagan would say after leaving office. "I have to tell you, I enjoyed it."

▲ **THE TROIKA:** *From left to right,* James Baker III, chief of staff; Edwin Meese III, counselor to the president; and Michael Deaver, deputy chief of staff. Baker, a shrewd Texas lawyer, ran the executive office of the president—the staff numbered some 800—and negotiated with Congress. Meese, also a lawyer, served as Reagan's conservative conscience, making certain that administration policy conformed with the chief executive's principles. Deaver, a public relations man, managed the president's schedule, press appearances, and public image. They remained in the White House throughout the first term.

▶ **CLASS PHOTO:** Two weeks into the new administration, Reagan's cabinet in the Oval Office. *Front row (L–R):* Alexander Haig (State), President Ronald Reagan, Vice President George H. W. Bush, and Caspar Weinberger (Defense). *Behind (L–R):* Raymond Donovan (Labor), Donald Regan (Treasury), Terrel Bell (Education), David Stockman (Office of Management and Budget), Andrew Lewis (Transportation), Samuel Pierce (Housing and Urban Development), William French Smith (Justice), James Watt (Interior), Jeane Kirkpatrick (U.N. ambassador), Edwin Meese III (counselor to the president), James Edwards (Energy), Malcolm Baldrige (Commerce), William E. Brock (U.S. trade representative), Richard Schweiker (Health and Human Services), John Block (Agriculture), and William Casey (Central Intelligence).

▶ **HOME AT LAST:** The White House reception for the American hostages who had been held in Iran. The date is January 27, 1981, just one week after Reagan took the oath of office and the hostages were released. "I'm told that Sergeant Lopez here put up a sign in his cell, a sign that normally would have been torn down by...guards," the president said. "But this one was written in Spanish, and his guards didn't know that '*Viva la roja, blanco, y azul*' means 'Long live the red, white, and blue.' They may not understand what that means in Iran, but we do, Sergeant Lopez, and you've filled our hearts with pride."

▲ **POLITICAL SOUL MATES:** The president and British Prime Minister Margaret Thatcher on the South Lawn reviewing troops, February 26, 1981. Reagan and Thatcher saw each other as political soul mates. "We had a private meeting in Oval office [sic]," Reagan would write in his diary. "[S]he is as firm as ever re the Soviets and for reduction of govt."

◄ **HAPPY BIRTHDAY, MR. PRESIDENT:** Not quite three weeks after taking the oath of office, the president turned 70. In the morning, Speaker of the House Tip O'Neill gave him a cake. That evening, the first lady threw this party. As crooner Frank Sinatra dances with Nancy, the Gipper tries to cut in on Ol' Blue Eyes.

▲ **THE MOMENT BEFORE:** Leaving the Washington Hilton after giving a luncheon address to AFL-CIO representatives, the president waves to onlookers. In the next moment, two shots rang out. Reacting instantly, Secret Service agents lunged toward the president. Then, as three more shots sounded, the agents shoved him into his limousine. The fifth bullet struck the limousine, flattened to the thickness of a dime, and slipped through the open door, entering the president's body through his left armpit. The bullet ripped through Reagan's lung, coming to rest an inch from his heart.

▲ **THE MOMENT AFTER:** By the time this photograph was snapped, the assailant, John Hinckley, had been wrestled to the ground, and the motorcade surrounding the president's limousine had raced off, lights flashing and sirens blaring, in the direction of the George Washington University Hospital. On the ground are Thomas Delahanty, a Washington policeman who was shot in the neck, and James Brady, the White House press secretary, who was shot in the head. Although not pictured, Secret Service agent Tim McCarthy was also shot, becoming one of only two agents to ever take a bullet for a president. All three survived. Brady, who became an anti–gun violence advocate, was confined to a wheelchair for life.

▲ **THE SITUATION ROOM:** As surgeons operated on the president and Vice President Bush flew back to Washington from Texas, senior members of the administration met in the White House Situation Room to determine whether the attempt on the president's life represented an isolated act or was part of a larger effort to undermine the government. *From left to right:* Helene von Damm, director of presidential personnel; Fred Fielding, counsel to the president; Andrew Lewis, secretary of transportation; Richard Allen, national security advisor; Donald Regan, secretary of the treasury; Alexander Haig, secretary of state; David Gergen, director of communications; Max Friedersdorf, congressional liaison; Larry Speakes of the press office; Richard Darman, assistant to the president; and Caspar Weinberger, secretary of defense.

◀ **IN CONTROL HERE:** At one point, Secretary of State Alexander Haig left the Situation Room to speak to reporters. "Constitutionally, gentlemen," Haig said, "you have the president, the vice president, and the secretary of state, in that order... As of now, I am in control here, in the White House, pending return of the vice president..." Although he accurately described the chain of command in the executive branch, Haig appeared to have misstated the presidential line of succession, in which the speaker of the House and then the president pro tempore of the Senate—not the secretary of state—follow the vice president. Instead of reassuring the nation, Haig unnerved it.

BUSS STOP: Although his physician would judge the president's recovery incomplete until October, some six months after he was shot, Reagan would address a joint session of Congress in April, less than a month after the attempt on his life, and then, in mid-May, travel to Indiana to deliver the commencement address at Notre Dame. Here we see the chief executive in the Oval Office in June, 1981, hale enough to accept busses from Miss Universe Shawn Weatherly and Miss USA Kim Seelbrede.

RECOVERY PLAN: Still recovering at the George Washington University Hospital, a wan Ronald Reagan smiles at a huge get-well card from his staff, who posed on the steps of the Old Executive Office Building, the elaborate 19th-century building next to the White House. On April 12, 1981, just four days after this photograph was taken, the president returned to the White House. "Whatever happens now," Reagan would write in his diary, "I owe my life to God and will try to serve him in every way I can."

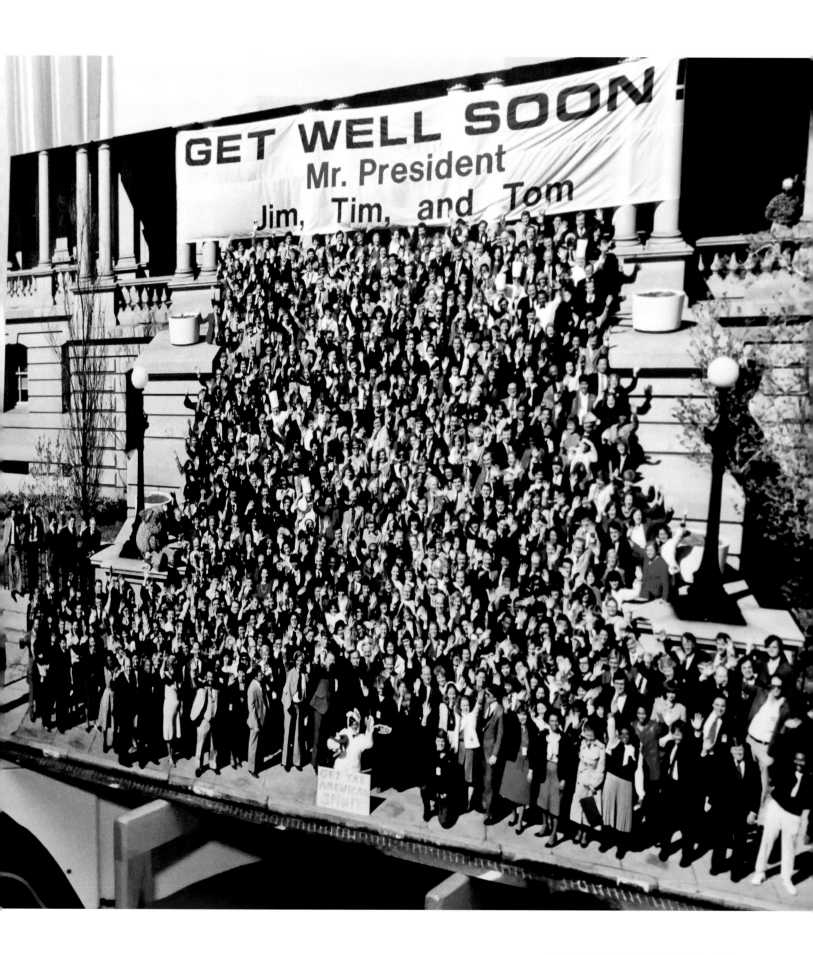

Government...has to provide without interruption the protective services which are its reason for being.

—REMARKS ON THE AIR TRAFFIC CONTROLLERS STRIKE, AUGUST 3, 1981

▶ **STRIKEBREAKER:** On August 3, 1981, the roughly 13,000 members of the Professional Air Traffic Controllers Organization (PATCO) walked off their jobs, violating a law against strikes by government unions. Even though PATCO supported him during the 1980 campaign, Reagan, in the Rose Garden press conference pictured here, declared that if the air traffic controllers failed to return to work within 48 hours, "they have forfeited their jobs." Only about 1,300 came back. Reagan shocked the union by promptly firing the rest (and banning them from federal service for life). A former union head himself, Reagan took no pleasure in the act—"I'm sorry," he said, "and I'm sorry for them"—but in one move the new president demonstrated that he meant what he said. Attorney General William French Smith stands to Reagan's right.

▶ TAX CUTTER: On July 29, 1981, Congress enacted the centerpiece of Reagan's first-term economic program, the Economic Recovery Tax Act. (ERTA was also known as the Kemp-Roth bill, after Congressman Jack Kemp and Senator William Roth, who sponsored it.) "The whole day was given to phone calls to Congressmen," Reagan would write in his diary. "I went from fearing the worst to hope we'd squeak through." By late afternoon, both the Senate and House passed the legislation by large margins. Here the vice president and others join the president in the Oval Office to celebrate.

▶▶ FOGGY MORNING IN AMERICA (FOLLOWING PAGES): At his beloved Rancho del Cielo, the president signs the Economic Recovery Tax Act. Phasing in reductions over three years, ERTA reduced marginal income tax rates by 23 percent. ERTA also cut the top income tax rate from 70 to 50 percent and mandated that, beginning in 1985, income tax rates would be indexed for inflation. All in all, ERTA represented one of the largest tax cuts in American history.

EDITOR: At his desk in the Oval Office, President Reagan works on a draft of an address to the nation on the economy. September 24, 1981.

WOMEN'S ADVOCATE: President Reagan poses with the nine justices of the Supreme Court, including his appointee, Justice Sandra Day O'Connor, the first woman named to the high court. September 25, 1981.

EXECUTIVE: In the Situation Room, President Reagan presides over a meeting called to weigh the implications of the death of President Anwar Sadat of Egypt, assassinated by Islamic radicals earlier that day. October 6, 1981.

MEMBERS OF THE CLUB: In the White House Blue Room, President Reagan hosts three men who occupied the presidency before him and one who would occupy it afterward. Former presidents Nixon, Carter, and Ford and Vice President George H. W. Bush would lead the American delegation to the funeral of assassinated Egyptian president Anwar Sadat. October 8, 1981.

▲ **QUARTERBACK-IN-CHIEF:** The chief executive, in the Oval Office, poses with a USC football on March 26, 1982, just four days short of the first anniversary of the attempt on his life. "My father was a very physical person," Ron Reagan would observe later. "While he was never big or strong or fast enough to be a professional athlete, there was just this innate athleticism to him. He was at ease with his own body."

▶ **STRONGMAN:** After the assassination attempt, Reagan began working out with weights each evening to regain his strength. Enjoying these workouts, he kept at them—soon adding an inch to the circumference of his chest. In the East Room on February 2, 1982, just four days before his 71st birthday, the president delightedly shows off. Also in the picture, legendary NFL coach George Allen, a member of the President's Council on Physical Fitness and Sports.

◄ **EASY RIDERS:** On March 4, 1982, their 30th wedding anniversary, the president and the first lady celebrate by trying out an anniversary gift, a riding mower with the presidential seal on the hood. Whenever he visited the ranch, Reagan would perform hard physical labor for hours at a time, clearing trails, pruning trees, or setting fence posts. "He'd come out one morning," recalled Dennis LeBlanc, the former state trooper who worked alongside Reagan, "and he'd say, 'Boy, I was able to pull in a notch on my belt on this trip.'"

France and America may not always see eye to eye on every issue, but we usually can. And like true friends, we know we can count on each other in times of peril.

—TOAST HONORING FRENCH PRESIDENT FRANÇOIS MITTERRAND, OCTOBER 18, 1981

▶ **FRENCH CONNECTION:** On June 6, 1982, the anniversary of D-Day, the president and the first lady attend a state dinner at Versailles. During this first trip abroad as president, Reagan took pains to prove to our allies that he was no warmonger— but that he was serious about keeping the Soviet Union under increasing pressure. "[D]inner in the Hall of Mirrors," Reagan would write in his diary. "[T]he table had to be at least 100 feet long—an unbelievably beautiful sight."

▲ ANTI-COMMUNIST CRUSADERS: At the Vatican, June 7, 1982. Three years earlier, on his first papal visit to his native Poland, the pope had drawn crowds that numbered in the millions, rebuking the Communist regime. Ronald Reagan, then a presidential candidate, had watched the pontiff's visit with tears in his eyes. Both men of faith, both opposed to communism, both survivors of assassination attempts, and both former actors, the president and the pope meet here for the first time. They would work together throughout the Reagan presidency.

▲ **FELLOW EQUESTRIANS:** The president with Queen Eliza-beth II at Windsor Castle, June 8, 1982. While the queen took the president riding, Prince Philip, a champion carriage driver, took the first lady for a ride around Windsor Great Park in a coach-and-four. "[A] fairy-tale visit with…the royal family," Reagan would later write. "I must admit, the queen is quite an accomplished horsewoman."

◀◀ A PARLIAMENTARY ADDRESS (PREVIOUS PAGES): After riding in Windsor, Reagan traveled to London, where he became the first president of the United States (and only the second non-British head of state) to address a joint session of Parliament. "In an ironic sense Karl Marx was right," Reagan said. "We are witnessing today a great revolutionary crisis... But the crisis is happening not in the free, non-Marxist West, but in the home of Marxist-Leninism, the Soviet Union... [T]he march of freedom and democracy... will leave Marxism-Leninism on the ash-heap of history."

▶ HOMECOMING: For much of his married life, Reagan spent a lot of time away from home, giving speeches, filming movies or television programs, and making public appearances. Once he became president, though, he and Nancy reveled in each other's company. Whenever their schedules permitted, they would spend weekday evenings alone together in the private quarters of the White House, watching television while doing paperwork. On weekends, Marine One would fly them to Camp David. Although he sometimes held staff meetings at the presidential retreat, Reagan reserved most of his time at Camp David for Nancy. In this photograph, taken on September 12, 1982, the president and first lady have just returned from Camp David, stepping from the presidential helicopter onto the South Lawn. A portrait of one of the very few first couples to look upon the presidency as a chance to spend more time together.

◄ **SURPRISE PARTY:** At the lectern in the White House press room on February 4, 1983, the chief executive, about to turn 72, fields questions from reporters. Peeking around the corner, the first lady, backed by communications director David Gergen, prepares to surprise him. In this photograph by Reagan's personal photographer, Michael Evans, note Nancy's unfeigned delight.

▲ **FREEDOM FIGHTER:** In December 1979, the Soviet Union invaded Afghanistan. Determined to support the Afghan resistance, Reagan increased U.S. support for the anti-Soviet mujahideen. Here, in the Oval Office on February 2, 1983, the president meets with Afghan warriors. The Soviets would begin withdrawing from Afghanistan some five years later. In effect, the Reagan Doctrine, which held that the United States would help opponents of Soviet domination, overcame the Brezhnev Doctrine, which stipulated that no country would ever be permitted to leave the Soviet orbit.

▲ **ON THE SCENE:** As flood levels of the Ouachita River rise in January 1983, the president tours Monroe, Louisiana, where volunteers had worked for hours on end. "The entire country has watched the volunteers who have been filling and stacking sandbags," Reagan said in a radio address soon afterward. "You exemplify the concept of neighbor helping neighbor, which is the very basis of our way of life."

REMARKS AT THE ANNUAL CONVENTION OF THE NATIONAL ASSOCIATION OF EVANGELICALS

March 8, 1983

In this address, delivered in Orlando, Florida, Ronald Reagan laid out the moral case against communism. Although he was sometimes accused of catering to, or indulging, evangelical Christians, note that here Reagan instead admonishes them: "[I]n your discussions of the nuclear freeze proposals, I urge you to beware the temptation of pride—the temptation of blithely declaring yourselves above it all and labeling both sides equally at fault, to ignore the facts of history and the aggressive impulses of an evil empire."

Those of you in the National Association of Evangelicals[1] are known for your spiritual and humanitarian work. And I would be especially remiss if I didn't discharge right now one personal debt of gratitude. Thank you for your prayers. Nancy and I have felt their presence many times in many ways. And believe me, for us, they've made all the difference.

---

[1] A religious organization, founded in 1942, that today represents approximately 40 Christian denominations and 45,000 churches in the United States.

The other day in the East Room of the White House at a meeting there, someone asked me whether I was aware of all the people out there who were praying for the president. And I had to say, "Yes, I am. I've felt it. I believe in intercessionary prayer."[2] But I couldn't help but say to that questioner, after he'd asked the question, that—or at least say to them that if sometimes when he was praying he got a busy signal, it was just me in there ahead of him. I think I understand how Abraham Lincoln felt when he said, "I have been driven many times to my knees by the overwhelming conviction that I had nowhere else to go."

From the joy and the good feeling of this conference, I go to a political reception. Now, I don't know why, but that bit of scheduling reminds me of a story, which I'll share with you.

An evangelical minister and a politician arrived at heaven's gate one day together. And Saint Peter, after doing all the necessary formalities, took them in hand to show them where their quarters would be. And he took them to a small, single room with a bed, a chair, and a table and said this was for the clergyman. And the politician was a little worried about what might be in store for him. And he couldn't believe it then when Saint Peter stopped in front of a beautiful mansion with lovely grounds, many servants, and told him that these would be his quarters.

And he couldn't help but ask, he said, "But wait, how—there's something wrong—how do I get this mansion while that good and holy man only gets a single room?" And Saint Peter said, "You have to understand how things are up here. We've got thousands and thousands of clergy. You're the first politician who ever made it."

But I don't want to contribute to a stereotype. So I tell you there are a great many God-fearing, dedicated, noble men and women in public life, present company included. And, yes, we need your help to keep us ever mindful of the ideas and the principles that brought us into the public arena in the first place. The basis of those ideals and principles is a commitment to freedom and personal liberty that, itself, is grounded in the much deeper realization that freedom prospers only where the blessings of God are avidly sought and humbly accepted.

The American experiment in democracy rests on this insight. Its discovery was

---

[2] Often called "intercessory prayer," a form of prayer during which one or more people intercede or plead with God on behalf of another.

the great triumph of our Founding Fathers, voiced by William Penn when he said, "If we will not be governed by God, we must be governed by tyrants."[3] Explaining the inalienable rights of men, Jefferson said, "The God who gave us life, gave us liberty at the same time." And it was George Washington who said that "of all the dispositions and habits which lead to political prosperity, religion and morality are indispensable supports."

And finally, that shrewdest of all observers of American democracy, Alexis de Tocqueville, put it eloquently after he had gone on a search for the secret of America's greatness and genius—and he said, "Not until I went into the churches of America and heard her pulpits aflame with righteousness did I understand the greatness and the genius of America… America is good. And if America ever ceases to be good, America will cease to be great."[4]

Well, I'm pleased to be here today with you who are keeping America great by keeping her good. Only through your work and prayers and those of millions of others can we hope to survive this perilous century and keep alive this experiment in liberty, this last, best hope of man.

> Only through your work and prayers can we hope to survive this perilous century and keep alive this experiment in liberty, this last, best hope of man.

I want you to know that this administration is motivated by a political philosophy that sees the greatness of America in you, her people, and in your families, churches, neighborhoods, communities—the institutions that foster and nourish values like concern for others and respect for the rule of law under God.

---

[3] This quotation is most often attributed to William Penn (1644-1718), a Quaker dissident and the "proprietor" of the province of Pennsylvania, which he founded as a refuge from British religious intolerance. Cited by many modern writers and orators in a plethora of different forms, the quotation is most commonly rendered as, "Those people who will not be governed by God will be ruled by tyrants." In 1984, President Reagan officially proclaimed Penn and his second wife, Hannah, "honorary citizens of the United States."

[4] Although commonly attributed to the French historian and political thinker Alexis de Tocqueville (1805-1859), these words do not appear in de Tocqueville's *Democracy in America*.

Now, I don't have to tell you that this puts us in opposition to, or at least out of step with, a prevailing attitude of many who have turned to a modern-day secularism, discarding the tried and time-tested values upon which our very civilization is based. No matter how well intentioned, their value system is radically different from that of most Americans. And while they proclaim that they're freeing us from superstitions of the past, they've taken upon themselves the job of superintending us by government rule and regulation. Sometimes their voices are louder than ours, but they are not yet a majority.

An example of that vocal superiority is evident in a controversy now going on in Washington. And since I'm involved, I've been waiting to hear from the parents of young America. How far are they willing to go in giving to government their prerogatives as parents?

Let me state the case as briefly and simply as I can. An organization of citizens,[5] sincerely motivated and deeply concerned about the increase in illegitimate births and abortions involving girls well below the age of consent, some time ago established a nationwide network of clinics to offer help to these girls and, hopefully, alleviate this situation. Now, again, let me say, I do not fault their intent. However, in their well-intentioned effort, these clinics have decided to provide advice and birth control drugs and devices to underage girls without the knowledge of their parents.

For some years now, the federal government has helped with funds to subsidize these clinics. In providing for this, the Congress decreed that every effort would be made to maximize parental participation. Nevertheless, the drugs and devices are prescribed without getting parental consent or giving notification after they've done so. Girls termed "sexually active"—and that has replaced the word "promiscuous"— are given this help in order to prevent illegitimate birth or abortion.

Well, we have ordered clinics receiving federal funds to notify the parents [that] such help has been given. One of the nation's leading newspapers[6] has created the term "squeal rule" in editorializing against us for doing this, and we're being criticized for violating the privacy of young people. A judge has recently granted an injunction against an enforcement of our rule. I've watched TV panel shows discuss

[5] The Planned Parenthood Federation of America (founded as the American Birth Control League in 1923).

[6] *The New York Times,* February 11, 1983.

this issue, seen columnists pontificating on our error, but no one seems to mention morality as playing a part in the subject of sex.

Is all of Judeo-Christian tradition wrong? Are we to believe that something so sacred can be looked upon as a purely physical thing with no potential for emotional and psychological harm? And isn't it the parents' right to give counsel and advice to keep their children from making mistakes that may affect their entire lives?

Many of us in government would like to know what parents think about this intrusion in their family by government. We're going to fight in the courts. The right of parents and the rights of family take precedence over those of Washington-based bureaucrats and social engineers.

But the fight against parental notification is really only one example of many attempts to water down traditional values and even abrogate the original terms of American democracy. Freedom prospers when religion is vibrant and the rule of law under God is acknowledged. When our Founding Fathers passed the First Amendment, they sought to protect churches from government interference. They never intended to construct a wall of hostility between government and the concept of religious belief itself.

> Freedom prospers when religion is vibrant and the rule of law under God is acknowledged.

The evidence of this permeates our history and our government. The Declaration of Independence mentions the Supreme Being no less than four times. "In God We Trust" is engraved on our coinage. The Supreme Court opens its proceedings with a religious invocation. And the members of Congress open their sessions with a prayer. I just happen to believe the schoolchildren of the United States are entitled to the same privileges as Supreme Court justices and congressmen.

Last year, I sent the Congress a constitutional amendment to restore prayer to public schools. Already this session, there's growing bipartisan support for the amendment, and I am calling on the Congress to act speedily to pass it and to let our children pray.

Perhaps some of you read recently about the Lubbock school case, where a judge actually ruled that it was unconstitutional for a school district to give equal treatment to religious and nonreligious student groups, even when the group meetings were being held during the students' own time. The First Amendment never intended to require government to discriminate against religious speech.

Senators Denton[7] and Hatfield[8] have proposed legislation in the Congress on the whole question of prohibiting discrimination against religious forms of student speech. Such legislation could go far to restore freedom of religious speech for public school students. And I hope the Congress considers these bills quickly. And with your help, I think it's possible we could also get the constitutional amendment through the Congress this year.

> Unless and until it can be proven that the unborn child is not a living entity, then its right to life, liberty, and the pursuit of happiness must be protected.

More than a decade ago, a Supreme Court decision literally wiped off the books of 50 states statutes protecting the rights of unborn children. Abortion on demand now takes the lives of up to one and a half million unborn children a year. Human life legislation ending this tragedy will someday pass the Congress, and you and I must never rest until it does. Unless and until it can be proven that the unborn child is not a living entity, then its right to life, liberty, and the pursuit of happiness must be protected.

You may remember that when abortion on demand began, many—and, indeed, I'm sure, many of you—warned that the practice would lead to a decline in respect for human life, that the philosophical premises used to justify abortion on demand would ultimately be used to justify other attacks on the sacredness of human life—infanticide or mercy killing. Tragically enough, those warnings proved all too true.

---

[7] Admiral Jeremiah Denton (b. 1924) was a one-term Republican senator from Alabama from 1981 to 1987.

[8] Mark Hatfield (b. 1922) was a Republican senator from Oregon from 1967 to 1997. At the time of this speech, he was chairman of the powerful Senate Committee on Appropriations.

Only last year, a court permitted the death by starvation of a handicapped infant.[9]

I have directed the Health and Human Services Department to make clear to every health care facility in the United States that the Rehabilitation Act of 1973 protects all handicapped persons against discrimination based on handicaps, including infants. And we have taken the further step of requiring that each and every recipient of federal funds who provides health care services to infants must post, and keep posted in a conspicuous place, a notice stating that "discriminatory failure to feed and care for handicapped infants in this facility is prohibited by federal law." It also lists a 24-hour toll-free number so that nurses and others may report violations in time to save the infant's life.

In addition, recent legislation introduced in the Congress by Representative Henry Hyde of Illinois not only increases restrictions on publicly financed abortions; it also addresses this whole problem of infanticide.[10] I urge the Congress to begin hearings and to adopt legislation that will protect the right of life to all children, including the disabled or handicapped.

Now, I'm sure that you must get discouraged at times, but you've done better than you know, perhaps. There's a great spiritual awakening in America, a renewal of the traditional values that have been the bedrock of America's goodness and greatness.

One recent survey by a Washington-based research council concluded that Americans were far more religious than the people of other nations; 95 percent of those surveyed expressed a belief in God, and a huge majority believed the Ten Commandments had real meaning in their lives. And another study has found that an overwhelming majority of Americans disapprove of adultery, teenage sex, pornography, abortion, and hard drugs. And this same study showed a deep reverence for the importance of family ties and religious belief.

I think the items that we've discussed here today must be a key part of the nation's political agenda. For the first time the Congress is openly and seriously debating and dealing with the prayer and abortion issues—and that's enormous

[9] On April 9, 1982, a baby known as Infant Doe was born with Down syndrome and another condition that is fatal if not surgically repaired. Infant Doe's parents would not consent to an operation, and the baby died of starvation six days later. See Daryl Evans, "The Psychological Impact of Disability and Illness on Medical Treatment Decision-making," *Issues in Law & Medicine*, December 22, 1989.

[10] Representative Hyde (1924-2007) was also the author of the Hyde Amendment, first enacted in 1976, which barred the use of Department of Health and Human Services funds to pay for abortions.

progress right there. I repeat: America is in the midst of a spiritual awakening and a moral renewal. And with your biblical keynote, I say today, "Yes, let justice roll on like a river, righteousness like a never-failing stream."[11]

> There is sin and evil in the world, and we're enjoined by Scripture and the Lord Jesus to oppose it with all our might. The glory of this land has been its capacity for transcending the moral evils of our past.

Now, obviously, much of this new political and social consensus I've talked about is based on a positive view of American history, one that takes pride in our country's accomplishments and record. But we must never forget that no government schemes are going to perfect man. We know that living in this world means dealing with what philosophers would call the phenomenology of evil or, as theologians would put it, the doctrine of sin.

There is sin and evil in the world, and we're enjoined by Scripture and the Lord Jesus to oppose it with all our might. Our nation, too, has a legacy of evil with which it must deal. The glory of this land has been its capacity for transcending the moral evils of our past. For example, the long struggle of minority citizens for equal rights, once a source of disunity and civil war, is now a point of pride for all Americans. We must never go back. There is no room for racism, anti-Semitism, or other forms of ethnic and racial hatred in this country.

I know that you've been horrified, as have I, by the resurgence of some hate groups preaching bigotry and prejudice. Use the mighty voice of your pulpits and the powerful standing of your churches to denounce and isolate these hate groups in our midst. The commandment given us is clear and simple: "Thou shalt love thy neighbor as thyself."

---

[11] Amos 5:24.

But whatever sad episodes exist in our past, any objective observer must hold a positive view of American history, a history that has been the story of hopes fulfilled and dreams made into reality. Especially in this century, America has kept alight the torch of freedom, but not just for ourselves but for millions of others around the world.

And this brings me to my final point today. During my first press conference as president, in answer to a direct question, I pointed out that, as good Marxist-Leninists, the Soviet leaders have openly and publicly declared that the only morality they recognize is that which will further their cause, which is world revolution. I think I should point out I was only quoting Lenin, their guiding spirit, who said in 1920 that they repudiate all morality that proceeds from supernatural ideas—that's their name for religion—or ideas that are outside class conceptions. Morality is entirely subordinate to the interests of class war. And everything is moral that is necessary for the annihilation of the old, exploiting social order and for uniting the proletariat.

> There is no room for racism, anti-Semitism, or other forms of ethnic and racial hatred in this country. Use the mighty voice of your pulpits to denounce and isolate these hate groups in our midst.

Well, I think the refusal of many influential people to accept this elementary fact of Soviet doctrine illustrates an historical reluctance to see totalitarian powers for what they are. We saw this phenomenon in the 1930s. We see it too often today.

This doesn't mean we should isolate ourselves and refuse to seek an understanding with them. I intend to do everything I can to persuade them of our peaceful intent, to remind them that it was the West that refused to use its nuclear monopoly in the '40s and '50s for territorial gain and which now proposes a 50 percent cut in strategic ballistic missiles and the elimination of an entire class of land-based, intermediate-range nuclear missiles.

At the same time, however, they must be made to understand we will never compromise our principles and standards. We will never give away our freedom. We will never abandon our belief in God. And we will never stop searching for a genuine peace. But we can assure none of these things America stands for through the so-called nuclear freeze solutions proposed by some. The truth is that a freeze now would be a very dangerous fraud, for that is merely the illusion of peace. The reality is that we must find peace through strength.

I would agree to a freeze if only we could freeze the Soviets' global desires. A freeze at current levels of weapons would remove any incentive for the Soviets to negotiate seriously in Geneva and virtually end our chances to achieve the major arms reductions which we have proposed. Instead, they would achieve their objectives through the freeze.

A freeze would reward the Soviet Union for its enormous and unparalleled military buildup. It would prevent the essential and long-overdue modernization of United States and allied defenses and would leave our aging forces increasingly vulnerable. And an honest freeze would require extensive prior negotiations on the systems and numbers to be limited and on the measures to ensure effective verification and compliance. And the kind of a freeze that has been suggested would be virtually impossible to verify. Such a major effort would divert us completely from our current negotiations on achieving substantial reductions.

A number of years ago, I heard a young father, a very prominent young man in the entertainment world, addressing a tremendous gathering in California. It was during the time of the Cold War, and communism and our own way of life were very much on people's minds. And he was speaking to that subject. And suddenly,

> We will never compromise our principles and standards. We will never give away our freedom. We will never abandon our belief in God.

though, I heard him saying, "I love my little girls more than anything." And I said to myself, "Oh, no, don't. You can't. Don't say that." But I had underestimated him. He went on: "I would rather see my little girls die now, still believing in God, than have them grow up under communism and one day die no longer believing in God."

There were thousands of young people in that audience. They came to their feet with shouts of joy. They had instantly recognized the profound truth in what he had said, with regard to the physical and the soul and what was truly important.

Yes, let us pray for the salvation of all of those who live in that totalitarian darkness. Pray they will discover the joy of knowing God. But until they do, let us be aware that while they preach the supremacy of the state, declare its omnipotence over individual man, and predict its eventual domination of all peoples on the earth, they are the focus of evil in the modern world.

It was C. S. Lewis[12] who, in his unforgettable *Screwtape Letters*,[13] wrote: "The greatest evil is not done now in those sordid 'dens of crime' that Dickens loved to paint. It is not even done in concentration camps and labor camps. In those we see its final result. But it is conceived and ordered (moved, seconded, carried, and minuted) in clear, carpeted, warmed, and well-lighted offices, by quiet men with white collars and cut fingernails and smooth-shaven cheeks who do not need to raise their voice."

Well, because these "quiet men" do not "raise their voices," because they sometimes speak in soothing tones of brotherhood and peace, because, like other dictators before them, they're always making "their final territorial demand," some would have us accept them at their word and accommodate ourselves to their aggressive impulses. But if history teaches anything, it teaches that simple-minded appeasement or wishful thinking about our adversaries is folly. It means the betrayal of our past, the squandering of our freedom.

So I urge you to speak out against those who would place the United States in a position of military and moral inferiority. You know, I've always believed that

---

[12] C. S. Lewis (1898-1963) was an Irish-born British novelist, academic, literary critic, essayist, and Christian apologist perhaps best known for his seven-book series *The Chronicles of Narnia*.

[13] *The Screwtape Letters* is composed of a series of fictional letters from a senior demon, Screwtape, to his nephew, advising him on the best methods of ensuring the damnation of a British man.

Old Screwtape reserved his best efforts for those of you in the church. So, in your discussions of the nuclear freeze proposals, I urge you to beware the temptation of pride—the temptation of blithely declaring yourselves above it all and label both sides equally at fault, to ignore the facts of history and the aggressive impulses of an evil empire, to simply call the arms race a giant misunderstanding and thereby remove yourself from the struggle between right and wrong and good and evil.

> Beware the temptation to ignore the facts of history and the aggressive impulses of an evil empire and thereby remove yourself from the struggle between right and wrong and good and evil.

I ask you to resist the attempts of those who would have you withhold your support for our efforts, this administration's efforts, to keep America strong and free while we negotiate real and verifiable reductions in the world's nuclear arsenals and, one day, with God's help, their total elimination.

While America's military strength is important, let me add here that I've always maintained that the struggle now going on for the world will never be decided by bombs or rockets, by armies or military might. The real crisis we face today is a spiritual one; at root, it is a test of moral will and faith.

Whittaker Chambers,[14] the man whose own religious conversion made him a witness to one of the terrible traumas of our time, the Hiss-Chambers case, wrote that the crisis of the Western world exists in the degree to which the West is indifferent to God, the degree to which it collaborates in communism's attempt to make man stand alone without God. And then he said, "For Marxism-Leninism is actually the second oldest faith,

[14] Whittaker Chambers (1901–1961) was a writer and editor for *Time* magazine and, later, William F. Buckley Jr.'s *National Review*. During the 1930s, he was both a member of the U.S. Communist Party and an admitted Soviet spy. He later renounced communism and denounced alleged fellow party members, including State Department official Alger Hiss, to the U.S. State Department and the House Un-American Activities Committee. Chambers's anti-Communist writing deeply influenced Reagan, who posthumously presented him with the Presidential Medal of Freedom in 1984.

first proclaimed in the Garden of Eden with the words of temptation 'Ye shall be as gods.'"[15]

The Western world can answer this challenge, he wrote, "but only provided that its faith in God and the freedom He enjoins is as great as communism's faith in Man."

I believe we shall rise to the challenge. I believe that communism is another sad, bizarre chapter in human history whose last pages even now are being written. I believe this because the source of our strength in the quest for human freedom is not material but spiritual. And because it knows no limitation, it must terrify and ultimately triumph over those who would enslave their fellow man. For in the words of Isaiah, "He giveth power to the faint … and to them that have no might … He increases strength … But they that wait upon the Lord … shall renew their strength. They shall mount up with wings as eagles. They shall run, and not be weary …"[16]

> I believe that communism is another sad, bizarre chapter in human history whose last pages even now are being written.

Yes, change your world. One of our Founding Fathers, Thomas Paine,[17] said, "We have it within our power to begin the world over again." We can do it, doing together what no one church could do by itself.

God bless you, and thank you very much.

[15] Genesis 3:5.

[16] Isaiah 40:29–31.

[17] Thomas Paine (1737–1809) wrote, among other things, the influential American revolutionary pamphlet *Common Sense*. He was a leading figure in both the American and the French revolutions.

We're a nation with global responsibilities. We're not somewhere else in the world protecting someone else's interests; we're there protecting our own.

—ADDRESS ON EVENTS IN LEBANON AND GRENADA, OCTOBER 27, 1983

▶ **PAYING TRIBUTE:** As the Lebanese civil war worsened, the United States joined Britain, France, and Italy in an attempt to restore order. Protesting the presence of American troops, a suicide bomber attacked the U.S. embassy in Beirut, killing 63. Five days later, on April 23, 1983, the Reagans drove to Andrews Air Force Base to honor the 17 Americans who numbered among the victims. "Nancy & I met individually with the families of the deceased," Reagan wrote in his diary that evening. "We were both in tears ... I was too choked up to speak."

▲ **THREE A.M. CALL:** While visiting the Augusta National Golf Club in Georgia on October 22, 1983, Reagan was awakened by a telephone call from Secretary of State George Shultz and National Security Advisor Robert McFarlane. Six nations in the Caribbean, they told him, had formally asked the United States to invade the Caribbean nation of Grenada. Internecine conflict within the governing Marxist clique on the tiny island had led to violence and instability. Reagan, conscious of the Cuban military presence on the island, thought for a moment, then spoke two words: "Do it." A few hours later, the president makes an early-morning call to monitor the situation.

▶ **GRENADA AND LEBANON:** On October 23, 1983, the day after the president approved the U.S. military intervention in Grenada, two car bombers attacked the American and French barracks in Beirut, killing 241 American and 58 French servicemen, a tragedy Reagan would later call the worst of his administration. Not quite 48 hours later, the invasion of Grenada began. Here, on October 27, Reagan edits the text of his address to the nation about both Lebanon and Grenada.

▲ **PHOTO OP:** Speaking from the Oval Office on January 29, 1984, the president made a brief address announcing that he and Vice President George Bush would run for reelection. Here, with the text of Reagan's remarks still on his desk, Nancy hugs the candidate. "The response has been terrific," Reagan, the working politician, wrote in his diary that evening. "[C]alls, wires, etc. running 10 to 1 in our favor."

◀ **LIT UP:** On December 15, 1983, the president lights the National Christmas Tree with help from Make-A-Wish Foundation beneficiary Amy Benham, who suffered from Hodgkin's disease. "If we live our lives for truth, for love, and for God," Reagan said in his remarks, "we never need be afraid."

Coming home to Nancy is like coming out of the cold into a warm, firelit room. I miss her if she just steps out of the room.

—*An American Life*, 1990

◄ **HAPPY LANDING:** Arriving at his California ranch on November 23, 1983, the president disembarks from Marine One. Nancy is there to greet him. Although it may have looked impressive in photographs, the house at Rancho del Cielo, like the houses on the other ranches Reagan once owned, was tiny and plain. As Reagan's son Ron would later recall, "the ranch house in Malibu was the kind of place where the foundation was collapsing and there was a hive of bees in the closet and dead bees all over the floor in the kids' room... Those ranches [were] one measure of my mother's love for my father."

Abraham Lincoln freed the black man. In many ways, Dr. King freed the white man... Where others—white and black—preached hatred, he taught the principles of love and nonviolence.

—Remarks on the birthday of Martin Luther King Jr., January 15, 1983

▶ **MLK HOLIDAY:** On November 2, 1983, flanked by, among others, Vice President Bush, Coretta Scott King, Representative Katie Hall of Indiana, and Senator Howard Baker, President Reagan signs into law the national holiday honoring Martin Luther King Jr. While arguing that King should be honored for lifting "the burden of racism," Reagan originally opposed the holiday, which gave federal workers another paid day off, as "too costly." As the legislation made its way through Congress, however, Reagan recognized what King meant to millions of Americans and reversed himself. "Often [Dr. King] was beaten [and] imprisoned," the president said at this signing ceremony, "but he never stopped teaching nonviolence. 'Work with the faith,' he told his followers, 'that unearned suffering is redemptive.'"

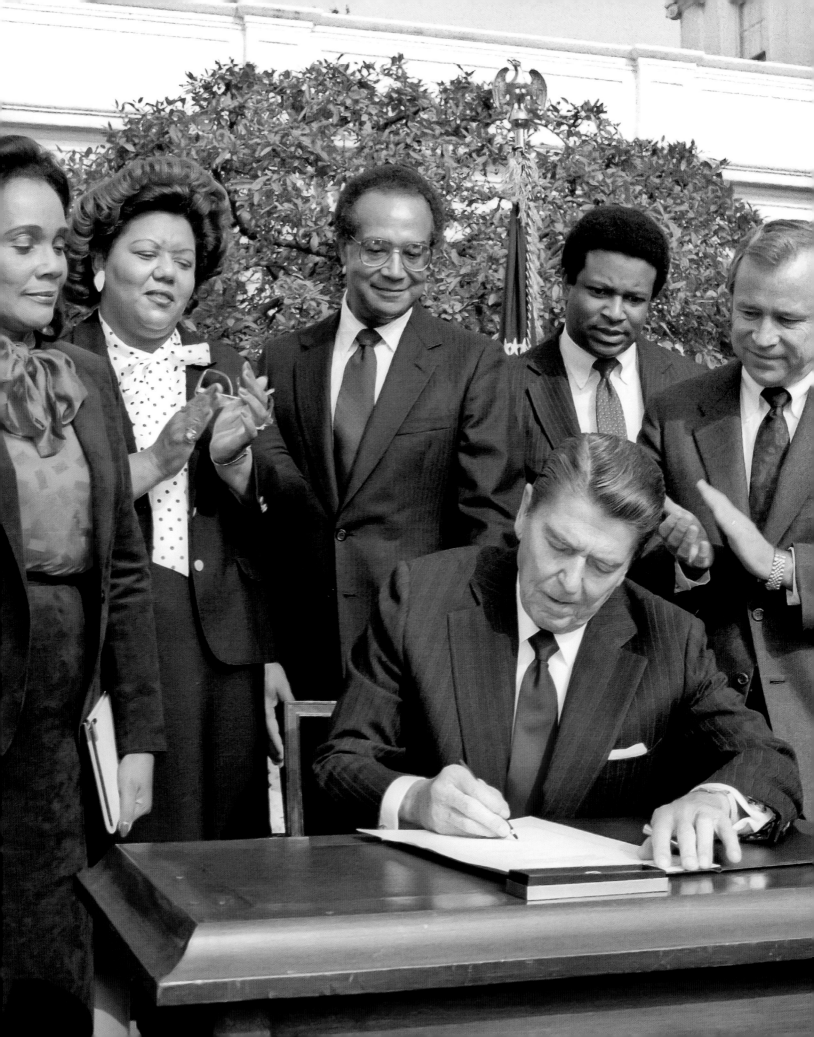

HALL-OF-FAMER: The New York Knicks' star seven-footer, Patrick Ewing, looms over the president and Senator Robert Dole, August 13, 1982.

KING OF POP: The president and the first lady emerge from the diplomatic entrance of the White House with pop royal Michael Jackson, May 14, 1985.

NOBEL PEACE LAUREATE: The president and first lady greet Mother Teresa of Calcutta in the Oval Office, June 20, 1985.

CHABADNIKS: The president receives a Hanukkah menorah from the Hassidic Friends of Lubavitch, December 15, 1987.

REMARKS AT A CEREMONY COMMEMORATING THE 40TH ANNIVERSARY OF THE NORMANDY INVASION

June 6, 1984

During the Normandy invasion, one of the most daunting assignments fell to U.S. Army Rangers: capturing the cliffs at Pointe du Hoc. Situated between the Omaha and Utah beaches, the guns on Pointe du Hoc threatened soldiers coming ashore on both. Under fire, taking heavy casualties, Rangers used rope ladders to scale the 100-foot cliffs. Forty years later, standing where the Rangers at last breasted the top, the president of the United States spoke in honor of those men and all those who came ashore in France that day. By then in their 60s, survivors of the assault on Pointe du Hoc joined the president at the event. Although Reagan took pride in keeping his emotions under control as he spoke, this time his eyes welled with tears. Also in attendance were representatives of each of the Allied nations, including Queen Elizabeth II of the United Kingdom, Queen Beatrix of the Netherlands, King Olav V of Norway, and King Baudouin of Belgium.

We're here to mark that day in history when the Allied armies joined in battle to reclaim this continent to liberty. For four long years, much of Europe had been under a terrible shadow. Free nations had fallen, Jews cried out in the camps, millions cried out for liberation. Europe was enslaved, and the world prayed for its rescue. Here in Normandy the rescue began. Here the Allies stood and fought against tyranny in a giant undertaking unparalleled in human history.

We stand on a lonely, windswept point on the northern shore of France. The air is soft, but 40 years ago at this moment, the air was dense with smoke and the cries of men, and the air was filled with the crack of rifle fire and the roar of cannon. At

dawn, on the morning of the 6th of June 1944, 225 Rangers[1] jumped off the British landing craft and ran to the bottom of these cliffs. Their mission was one of the most difficult and daring of the invasion: to climb these sheer and desolate cliffs and take out the enemy guns. The Allies had been told that some of the mightiest of these guns were here, and they would be trained on the beaches to stop the Allied advance.

There is a profound moral difference between the use of force for liberation and the use of force for conquest. You were here to liberate, not to conquer.

The Rangers looked up and saw the enemy soldiers [at] the edge of the cliffs, shooting down at them with machine guns and throwing grenades. And the American Rangers began to climb. They shot rope ladders over the face of these cliffs and began to pull themselves up. When one Ranger fell, another would take his place. When one rope was cut, a Ranger would grab another and begin his climb again. They climbed, shot back, and held their footing. Soon, one by one, the Rangers pulled themselves over the top, and in seizing the firm land at the top of these cliffs, they began to seize back the continent of Europe. Two hundred and twenty-five came here. After two days of fighting, only 90 could still bear arms.

Behind me is a memorial that symbolizes the Ranger daggers that were thrust into the top of these cliffs. And before me are the men who put them there. These are the boys of Pointe du Hoc. These are the men who took the cliffs. These are the champions who helped free a continent. These are the heroes who helped end a war.

Gentlemen, I look at you and I think of the words of Stephen Spender's poem.[2] You are men who in your "lives fought for life … and left the vivid air signed with your honor."

I think I know what you may be thinking right now—thinking, "We were just part of a bigger effort; everyone was brave that day." Well, everyone was. Do you

[1] Refers specifically, in this case, to the Second Ranger battalion, also known as Rudder's Rangers, after their commander, Colonel (later General) James Rudder (1910-1970), who was wounded twice during the operation.

[2] "I Think Continually of Those Who Were Truly Great" by the English poet, novelist, and essayist Sir Stephen Spender (1909-1995).

remember the story of Bill Millin of the 51st Highlanders? Forty years ago today, British troops were pinned down near a bridge, waiting desperately for help. Suddenly, they heard the sound of bagpipes, and some thought they were dreaming. Well, they weren't. They looked up and saw Bill Millin with his bagpipes, leading the reinforcements and ignoring the smack of the bullets into the ground around him.

Lord Lovat was with him—Lord Lovat of Scotland,[3] who calmly announced when he got to the bridge, "Sorry I'm a few minutes late," as if he'd been delayed by a traffic jam, when in truth he'd just come from the bloody fighting on Sword Beach, which he and his men had just taken.

There was the impossible valor of the Poles, who threw themselves between the enemy and the rest of Europe as the invasion took hold, and the unsurpassed courage of the Canadians, who had already seen the horrors of war on this coast. They knew what awaited them there, but they would not be deterred. And once they hit Juno Beach, they never looked back.

All of these men were part of a roll call of honor with names that spoke of a pride as bright as the colors they bore: the Royal Winnipeg Rifles, Poland's 24th Lancers, the Royal Scots Fusiliers, the Screaming Eagles,[4] the Yeomen of England's armored divisions, the forces of Free France, the Coast Guard's "Matchbox Fleet,"[5] and you, the American Rangers.

Forty summers have passed since the battle that you fought here. You were young the day you took these cliffs; some of you were hardly more than boys, with the deepest joys of life before you. Yet you risked everything here. Why? Why did you do it? What impelled you to put aside the instinct for self-preservation and risk your lives to take these cliffs? What inspired all the men of the armies that met here? We look at you, and somehow we know the answer. It was faith and belief; it was loyalty and love.

The men of Normandy had faith that what they were doing was right, faith that they fought for all humanity, faith that a just God would grant them mercy on this beachhead or on the next. It was the deep knowledge—and pray God we have not lost it—that there is a profound moral difference between the use of force

---

[3] Brigadier Simon Christopher Joseph Fraser, 15th Lord Lovat (1911-1995).

[4] The nickname of the U.S. 101st Airborne Division.

[5] A flotilla of sixty 83-foot wooden search-and-rescue Coast Guard cutters that cruised off all five landing beaches on D-Day and saved 400 Allied airmen and sailors.

for liberation and the use of force for conquest. You were here to liberate, not to conquer, and so you and those others did not doubt your cause. And you were right not to doubt.

You all knew that some things are worth dying for. One's country is worth dying for, and democracy is worth dying for, because it's the most deeply honorable form of government ever devised by man. All of you loved liberty. All of you were willing to fight tyranny, and you knew the people of your countries were behind you.

The Americans who fought here that morning knew word of the invasion was spreading through the darkness back home. They … felt in their hearts, though they couldn't know in fact, that in Georgia they were filling the churches at 4 a.m., in Kansas they were kneeling on their porches and praying, and in Philadelphia they were ringing the Liberty Bell.

Something else helped the men of D-day: their rock-hard belief that Providence would have a great hand in the events that would unfold here; that God was an ally in this great cause. And so, the night before the invasion, when Colonel Wolverton[6] asked his parachute troops to kneel with him in prayer, he told them, "Do not bow your heads, but look up so you can see God and ask His blessing in what we're about to do." Also that night, General Matthew Ridgway[7] on his cot, listening in the darkness for the promise God made to Joshua: "I will not fail thee nor forsake thee."[8]

These are the things that impelled them; these are the things that shaped the unity of the Allies.

When the war was over, there were lives to be rebuilt and governments to be returned to the people. There were nations to be reborn. Above all, there was a new peace to be assured. These were huge and daunting tasks. But the Allies summoned strength from the faith, belief, loyalty, and love of those who fell here. They rebuilt a new Europe together.

There was first a great reconciliation among those who had been enemies, all of whom had suffered so greatly. The United States did its part, creating the Marshall

[6] Lieutenant Colonel Robert Lee Wolverton (1914-1944) was the commander of the U.S. Third Battalion, 506th Parachute Infantry Regiment, 101st Airborne, from 1942 until his death on D-Day.

[7] Matthew Ridgway (1895-1993) was a U.S. general who commanded the 82nd Airborne Division during World War II. He later distinguished himself as commander of the Eighth Army during the Korean conflict. President Reagan awarded him the Presidential Medal of Freedom on May 12, 1986.

[8] Joshua 1:5.

Plan to help rebuild our allies and our former enemies. The Marshall Plan led to the Atlantic alliance—a great alliance that serves to this day as our shield for freedom, for prosperity, and for peace.

In spite of our great efforts and successes, not all that followed the end of the war was happy or planned. Some liberated countries were lost. The great sadness of this loss echoes down to our own time in the streets of Warsaw, Prague, and East Berlin. Soviet troops that came to the center of this continent did not leave when peace came. They're still there, uninvited, unwanted, unyielding, almost 40 years after the war. Because of this, allied forces still stand on this continent. Today, as 40 years ago, our armies are here for only one purpose—to protect and defend democracy. The only territories we hold are memorials like this one and graveyards where our heroes rest.

> We've learned that isolationism never was and never will be an acceptable response to tyrannical governments with expansionist intent.

We in America have learned bitter lessons from two world wars: It is better to be here, ready to protect the peace, than to take blind shelter across the sea, rushing to respond only after freedom is lost. We've learned that isolationism never was and never will be an acceptable response to tyrannical governments with an expansionist intent.

But we try always to be prepared for peace; prepared to deter aggression; prepared to negotiate the reduction of arms; and, yes, prepared to reach out again in the spirit of reconciliation. In truth, there is no reconciliation we would welcome more than a reconciliation with the Soviet Union, so [that] together we can lessen the risks of war now and forever.

It's fitting to remember here the great losses also suffered by the Russian people during World War II: 20 million perished, a terrible price that testifies to all the world the necessity of ending war. I tell you from my heart that we in the United States do not want war. We want to wipe from the face of the earth the terrible weapons that man now has in his hands. And I tell you, we are ready to seize that beachhead. We look for some sign from the Soviet Union that they are willing to move forward, that they share our desire and love for peace, and that they will give up the ways of conquest. There must be a changing there that will allow us to turn our hope into action.

I tell you from my heart that we in the United States do not want war. We want to wipe from the face of the earth the terrible weapons that man now has in his hands. And I tell you, we are ready to seize that beachhead.

We will pray forever that someday that changing will come. But for now, particularly today, it is good and fitting to renew our commitment to each other, to our freedom, and to the alliance that protects it.

We are bound today by what bound us 40 years ago—the same loyalties, traditions, and beliefs. We're bound by reality. The strength of America's allies is vital to the United States, and the American security guarantee is essential to the continued freedom of Europe's democracies. We were with you then; we are with you now. Your hopes are our hopes, and your destiny is our destiny.

Here, in this place where the West held together, let us make a vow to our dead. Let us show them by our actions that we understand what they died for. Let our actions say to them the words for which Matthew Ridgway listened: "I will not fail thee nor forsake thee."

Strengthened by their courage, heartened by their valor and borne by their memory, let us continue to stand for the ideals for which they lived and died.

Thank you very much, and God bless you all.

▲ **BAND OF BROTHERS:** The president greets former Army Rangers in Normandy, France. "These are the boys of Pointe du Hoc," Reagan said in his D-Day address. "These are the men who took the cliffs."

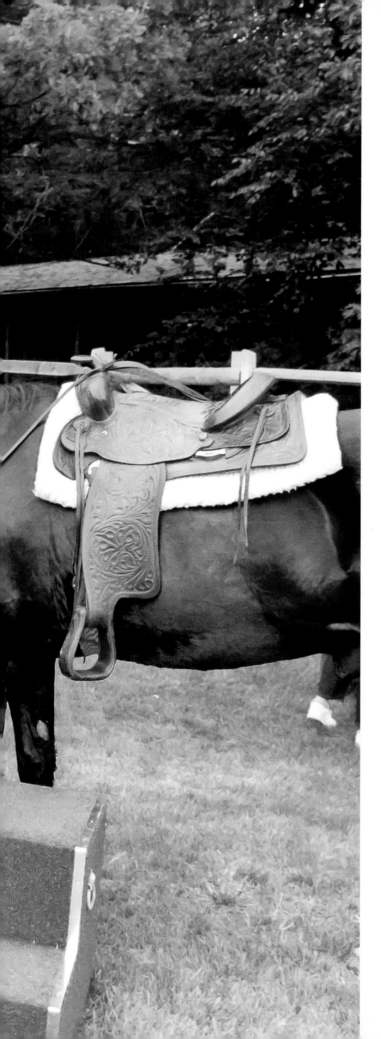

▲ **CLEAR-CUT:** The president of the United States at Rancho del Cielo, August 10, 1984. Clearing brush, pruning trees, digging postholes, splitting firewood, brushing down the horses, mucking out the stables, laboring for hours at a time while barely saying a word—Reagan loved hard physical work.

◄ **HORSING AROUND:** The Reagans at Camp David, July 21, 1984. Reagan joined a cavalry unit in the Army Reserve in 1937, and for the rest of his life he rode as often as he could. "Nothing is as good for the inside of man," he often quipped, "as the outside of a horse." Nancy never loved horses the way her husband did, but she learned to ride to keep him company.

►► **PROMISES KEPT (FOLLOWING PAGES):** The Republican National Convention, Dallas, Texas, August 23, 1984. With inflation down, tax cuts in place, and the economy expanding, Ronald Reagan accepts the Republican nomination for president for the second time. "In 1980," the president told the convention, "we asked the people of America, 'Are you better off than you were four years ago?' Well, the people answered then by choosing us to bring about a change. We have every reason now, four years later, to ask that same question again, for we have made a change."

▲ **THE ONCE AND FUTURE GOVERNOR:** At the Republican
National Convention in Dallas, August 23, 1984. Former California governor Ronald Reagan shakes hands with future governor and fellow actor Arnold Schwarzenegger, star of that year's
summer blockbuster *Terminator*.

▶ **WHISTLE-STOP:** In 1948 Reagan campaigned for the reelection of Democrat Harry Truman. Here, in 1984, Reagan
uses Truman's presidential railcar, the *Ferdinand Magellan*, to
campaign for his own reelection. "I know in a crowd this size
there must be many of you who are Democrats, as I once was,"
Reagan said in Sidney, Ohio. "You're not only welcome, but if
you are here, I think you're here because—like happened to me
once—you no longer can follow the policies of the leadership of
your party...Come on along with us."

▲ **CONCESSION CALL:** On election night, November 6, 1984, the president receives a concession call from former vice president Walter Mondale. Reagan defeated Mondale 59 to 41 percent in the popular vote, losing only Mondale's home state of Minnesota and the District of Columbia, for an electoral college victory of 525 to 13. Reagan's thumbs-up is an understatement. He and Vice President Bush had just won by the greatest electoral college margin in the history of the republic.

▶ **SECOND TERM:** In his private study off the Oval Office, the president works on his second inaugural address. This photograph was taken on January 17, 1985. Reagan was sworn in for his second term five days later. "At the heart of our efforts," he said, "is one idea vindicated by 25 straight months of economic growth: freedom and incentives unleash the drive and entrepreneurial genius that are the core of human progress." Looking over the president's shoulder, so to speak, are, among others, Prime Minister Margaret Thatcher, King Juan Carlos and Queen Sophia of Spain, King Hussein and Queen Noor of Jordan, German Chancellor Helmut Kohl, and Prince Phillip and Queen Elizabeth of Great Britain.

▲ **BIRTHDAY PORTRAIT:** Although Nancy was born on July 6, the Reagans celebrated her birthday each year in August, throwing a party during their sojourn at Rancho del Cielo. Here, on August 17, 1985, the family celebrates Nancy's 64th. From left, son Michael; the president with his grandson, Cameron; Michael's wife, Colleen, holding the hand of little Ashley Marie; the first lady; son Ron; Ron's wife, Doria; Patti's husband, Paul Grilley; and Patti. (Maureen and her husband, Dennis Revell, were unable to attend.)

◄ **ON THE LINE:** The president takes a call in the tack room at Rancho del Cielo, April 8, 1985. Reagan spent every August at the ranch, adding shorter visits as his schedule allowed. This photograph was taken during an eight-day stay. "[B]eautiful weather," he wrote in his diary, "a horseback ride every morning & wood cutting & brush hauling … in the afternoons." During his eight years in office, Reagan spent about a year of his presidency in the ranch house, not the White House.

▲ **STAR FOUR:** In the Indian Treaty Room of the Old Executive Office Building on June 13, 1986, the president and Senator Barry Goldwater present an honorary fourth star to 89-year-old General James "Jimmy" Doolittle. Doolittle, a lieutenant colonel in 1942, planned and led the famous "Doolittle Raid," during which 16 B-25s attacked Japan. Volunteering for the mission, Doolittle's raiders knew that, with too little fuel to return to an aircraft carrier, they would have to ditch their planes in Japanese-occupied China. Eleven crewmen were captured or killed, but the entire crews of 13 of the 16 aircraft, and all but one crewman in the 14th plane, eventually got home safely.

▲ **HIGH FIVE:** At the U.S. Naval Academy on May 22, 1985. "Four years ago, when you were entering Annapolis," the president said in his commencement address, "we were putting in place a program to rebuild America's weakened defenses, and I'm proud to say that much progress has been made. I know you're ready for the Navy, and I can tell you the Navy is now much more ready for you." The old cavalryman and a newly commissioned naval officer exchange a high five.

Surround yourself
with the best
people you can find,
delegate authority,
and don't interfere.

—*FORTUNE* MAGAZINE INTERVIEW,
SEPTEMBER 15, 1986

▶ **PRESIDENTIAL PUTT:** Flying to Geneva, Switzerland, on November 16, 1985, for his first summit meeting with Soviet General Secretary Mikhail Gorbachev. Instead of burying himself in briefing books, the president, his lightness of touch ever present, practices his putt. Those looking on include National Security Advisor Robert "Bud" McFarlane, in plaid; Secretary of State George Shultz, his elbow on the headrest of a chair; and, peeking over Shultz's shoulder, Chief of Staff Donald Regan. To preserve the crease in his trousers, Reagan has changed into sweatpants, his standard practice aboard Air Force One.

▲ IMAGE GAP: Moments after the Soviet leader climbs from his limousine, Ronald Reagan and General Secretary Mikhail Gorbachev pose for photographs. Reagan, dressed only in a suit despite the chill, exudes energy. Gorbachev, dressed in a coat and scarf and carrying a fedora of the kind that went out of style in the West three decades earlier, conveys an old-fashioned stiffness and discomfort. Although 20 years older than Gorbachev, Reagan appears more youthful and vigorous.

◄ THUMBS-UP: Geneva, Switzerland, November 19, 1985. Shortly before Mikhail Gorbachev arrives, Reagan gives the thumbs-up, displaying a sense of ease and self-confidence. Yet he felt the gravity of the moment. "[A] wakeful night," the president wrote in his diary the day before. "Lord I hope I'm ready & not overtrained."

▶▶ NOSE TO NOSE (FOLLOWING PAGES): The president and the general secretary meet at the Soviet mission during the second and final day of the Geneva summit, November 20, 1985. "Yes, we argued and we'd go nose to nose," Reagan would later say. "But when the argument was over, it was like it is with us [Americans]. He wasn't stalking out of there ... We fought it out ... but when the meeting was over we were normal."

The future doesn't belong to the fainthearted; it belongs to the brave.

—ADDRESS TO THE NATION ON THE
EXPLOSION OF THE SPACE SHUTTLE
CHALLENGER, JANUARY 28, 1986

▶ **CHALLENGER DISASTER:** The president and staffers, including White House Communications Director Pat Buchanan (second from right) and Chief of Staff Donald Regan (far right), watch the final moments of the space shuttle *Challenger,* January 28, 1986. Seventy-three seconds after takeoff, *Challenger* exploded and disintegrated above the Atlantic. The crew of seven, all of whom perished, included Christa McAuliffe, 37, a high school social studies teacher from Concord, New Hampshire, who had been selected as the first participant in the Teacher in Space program. That evening, less than six hours after *Challenger* exploded, President Reagan addressed the nation.

ADDRESS TO THE NATION ON THE EXPLOSION OF THE SPACE SHUTTLE CHALLENGER

January 28, 1986

On the morning of January 28, 1986, just 73 seconds after taking off from Kennedy Space Center, the space shuttle Challenger *broke apart, producing a twisting, erratic plume of smoke as it disintegrated above the Atlantic. All seven members of the crew perished, including Christa McAuliffe, a New Hampshire schoolteacher who had won a contest to become the first participant in the Teacher in Space Project. Scheduled to travel to the Capitol to deliver the State of the Union address that evening, President Reagan instead spoke to the nation from the Oval Office. "There is no way," he wrote in his diary, "to describe our shock & horror."*

Ladies and gentlemen, I'd planned to speak to you tonight to report on the state of the Union, but the events of earlier today have led me to change those plans. Today is a day for mourning and remembering. Nancy and I are pained to the core by the tragedy of the shuttle *Challenger*. We know we share this pain with all of the people of our country. This is truly a national loss.

Nineteen years ago, almost to the day, we lost three astronauts in a terrible accident on the ground. But we've never lost an astronaut in flight; we've never had a tragedy like this. And perhaps we've forgotten the courage it took for the crew of the shuttle. But they, the Challenger Seven, were aware of the dangers, but overcame them and did their jobs brilliantly. We mourn seven heroes: Michael Smith, Dick Scobee, Judith Resnik, Ronald McNair, Ellison Onizuka, Gregory Jarvis, and Christa McAuliffe. We mourn their loss as a nation together.

> We will never forget them, nor the last time we saw them, this morning, as they waved good-bye and "slipped the surly bonds of Earth" to "touch the face of God."

For the families of the seven, we cannot bear, as you do, the full impact of this tragedy. But we feel the loss, and we're thinking about you so very much. Your loved ones were daring and brave, and they had that special grace, that special spirit that says, "Give me a challenge, and I'll meet it with joy." They had a hunger to explore the universe and discover its truths. They wished to serve, and they did. They served all of us.

We've grown used to wonders in this century. It's hard to dazzle us. But for 25 years the United States space program has been doing just that. We've grown used to the idea of space, and perhaps we forget that we've only just begun. We're still pioneers. They, the members of the Challenger crew, were pioneers.

And I want to say something to the schoolchildren of America who were watching the live coverage of the shuttle's takeoff.[1] I know it is hard to understand, but sometimes painful things like this happen. It's all part of the process of exploration and discovery. It's all part of taking a chance and expanding man's horizons. The future doesn't belong to the fainthearted; it belongs to the brave. The *Challenger* crew was pulling us into the future, and

---

[1] Schoolteacher Christa McAuliffe, selected from more than 11,000 applicants to participate in the NASA Teacher in Space Project, was scheduled to teach two lessons from the *Challenger*. Schoolchildren across America were thus watching live on national television when the *Challenger* disintegrated.

we'll continue to follow them.

I've always had great faith in and respect for our space program, and what happened today does nothing to diminish it. We don't hide our space program. We don't keep secrets and cover things up. We do it all up front and in public. That's the way freedom is, and we wouldn't change it for a minute. We'll continue our quest in space. There will be more shuttle flights and more shuttle crews and, yes, more volunteers, more civilians, more teachers in space. Nothing ends here; our hopes and our journeys continue. I want to add that I wish I could talk to every man and woman who works for NASA or who worked on this mission and tell them: "Your dedication and professionalism have moved and impressed us for decades. And we know of your anguish. We share it."

There's a coincidence today. On this day 390 years ago, the great explorer Sir Francis Drake died aboard ship off the coast of Panama. In his lifetime the great frontiers were the oceans, and an historian later said, "He lived by the sea, died on it, and was buried in it." Well, today we can say of the *Challenger* crew: Their dedication was, like Drake's, complete.

The crew of the space shuttle *Challenger* honored us by the manner in which they lived their lives. We will never forget them, nor the last time we saw them, this morning, as they prepared for their journey and waved good-bye and "slipped the surly bonds of Earth" to "touch the face of God."[2]

[2] From the sonnet "High Flight" by John Gillespie Magee (1922-1941), an Anglo-American aviator and poet who served with the Royal Canadian Air Force and died in a midair collision over Lincolnshire, England, during World War II.

▲ **LIBERATOR:** On February 20, 1986, some two and a half years after the American invasion of the island, President Reagan visits Grenada, once again a functioning democracy. To his right, Prime Minister Herbert Blaize, whose party won the 1984 election. To his left, Paul Scoon, who, as governor general of the British Commonwealth nation, served as the representative of Queen Elizabeth II. During the invasion, Navy Special Forces freed Scoon from house arrest.

▲ **RETALIATOR:** In the Situation Room, April 15, 1986. Ten days earlier, Libyan agents had placed a bomb in a West Berlin nightclub frequented by U.S. servicemen, killing three patrons and injuring more than 200 others. Reagan retaliated by order-ing an air strike on Libya. In this photograph, General Charles Gabriel briefs the president, Secretary of State George Shultz, CIA Director William Casey, and others on the damage the strike inflicted.

"What can you say about a man who on Mother's Day sends flowers to his mother-in-law with a note thanking her for making him the happiest man on Earth?"

— NANCY REAGAN

▶ **THE BEACHCOMBERS:** Every American president since Franklin Roosevelt has visited Hawaii, and Ronald Reagan was no exception. En route to a six-day state visit to China, the president and first lady stopped off on Oahu, where they enjoyed the beachfront hospitality of resort mogul Chris Hemmeter. A bipartisan host, Hemmeter also provided accommodations for President Jimmy Carter.

◀ **BIG STICK:** New York Harbor, July 4, 1986, during celebrations marking the centennial of the Statue of Liberty, the president and the first lady stand at allegiance beneath the 16-inch guns of the USS *Iowa*—nicknamed "The Big Stick"—which was modernized as part of Reagan's plan for a 600-ship navy. "Call it mysticism if you will," Reagan said during his remarks the previous day, "[but] I have always believed there was some divine providence that placed this great land here between the two great oceans, to be found by a special kind of people from every corner of the world, who had a special love for freedom and a special courage."

▲ **SECOND SUMMIT:** President Reagan and Soviet General Secretary Gorbachev on the first day of their second summit in Reykjavik, Iceland. Gorbachev offered dramatic reductions in nuclear arms—but only if Reagan would agree to limit testing of the Strategic Defense Initiative, the research program designed to find ways to destroy nuclear missiles before they reached their targets. Reagan refused. When, on the second day of the summit, Gorbachev continued to insist, Reagan closed his briefing book, stood, and said, "The meeting is over."

▲ **NO DEAL:** Reagan and Gorbachev on October 12, 1986, moments after Reagan ended the final meeting—the faces of two men at an impasse. "I'd pledged that I wouldn't give away SDI & I didn't but that meant no deal," Reagan would write in his diary that evening. "I was mad—he tried to act jovial but I acted mad & it showed." Although it appeared to have failed, the Reykjavik summit proved a turning point, forcing the Soviets to recognize that they could never win the arms race. Visiting Russia several years later, former secretary of state Henry Kissinger asked officials to name the critical factor in the demise of the USSR. "Almost without exception," Kissinger said, "they named SDI."

◀ IRAN-CONTRA AFFAIR: In the Oval Office, November 25, 1986. The president discusses remarks about the Iran-contra affair with, from left, Defense Secretary Caspar Weinberger, Secretary of State George Shultz, Attorney General Edwin Meese III, and Chief of Staff Donald Regan.

In January 1986, on the advice of CIA Director William Casey and National Security Advisor John Poindexter, Reagan approved an arms sale to certain elements within the Iranian regime. He hoped to create an opening to moderates, who in turn agreed to use their influence to persuade their client, the Lebanese terrorist group, Hezbollah, to free six American hostages. When the arms deal became public, Reagan was accused of trading arms for hostages and diverting the proceeds to the contras, the anti-Communist resistance in Nicaragua. After spending more than seven years and $35 million investigating the Iran-contra affair, independent counsel Lawrence Walsh found "no credible evidence" that Reagan knew about the diversion of funds.

As for the arms deal, Reagan admitted in a televised address on March 4, 1987, that "what began as a strategic opening to Iran deteriorated, in its implementation, into trading arms for hostages. This runs counter to my own beliefs," said the president, "to administration policy, and to the original strategy we had in mind. There are reasons why it happened, but no excuses. It was a mistake."

REMARKS ON EAST-WEST RELATIONS AT THE BRANDENBURG GATE IN WEST BERLIN

June 12, 1987

While conducting research in West Berlin, the speechwriter who drafted this address (also the writer of this book) met a German woman, Ingeborg Elz. "If this man Gorbachev is serious with his talk of glasnost *and* perestroika," *she said when we discussed the Berlin Wall, "he can prove it. He can get rid of this wall." I adapted this remark, making the call to "tear down this wall" the centerpiece of the address. In a meeting in the Oval Office, President Reagan commented on the passage, noting that he particularly looked forward to delivering it. Then the address went to staffing. The National Security Council and the State Department opposed it, arguing that the call to tear down the wall would prove too provocative or confrontational. The president overruled them. The "boys at State" might disapprove, Reagan told me just before delivering the address, but "it's the right thing to do." On the night of November 9, 1989, two and a half years later, East Germany opened the checkpoints in the Berlin Wall. By the following morning, thousands had gathered at the structure, some singing and dancing atop the wall, others swinging picks and hammers at the tall concrete slabs of which it was composed. The wall had come down.*

Twenty-four years ago, President John F. Kennedy visited Berlin, speaking to the people of this city and the world at the city hall. Well, since then two other presidents have come, each in his turn, to Berlin. And today I myself make my second visit to your city.

We come to Berlin, we American presidents, because it's our duty to speak, in this place, of freedom. But I must confess, we're drawn here by other things as well: by the feeling of history in this city, more than 500 years older than our own nation; by the beauty of the Grunewald[1] and the Tiergarten[2]; most of all, by your courage and determination. Perhaps the composer Paul Lincke[3] understood something about American presidents. You see, like so many presidents before me, I come here today because wherever I go, whatever I do: *"Ich hab noch einen koffer in Berlin."*[4]

As long as this gate is closed, as long as this scar of a wall is permitted to stand, it is not the German question alone that remains open, but the question of freedom for all mankind.

Our gathering today is being broadcast throughout Western Europe and North America. I understand that it is being seen and heard as well in the East. To those listening throughout Eastern Europe, I extend my warmest greetings and the good will of the American people. To those listening in East Berlin, a special word: Although I cannot be with you, I address my remarks to you just as surely as to those standing here before me. For I join you, as I join your fellow countrymen in the West, in this firm, this unalterable belief: *Es gibt nur ein Berlin.*[5]

Behind me stands a wall that encircles the free sectors of this city, part of a vast system of barriers that divides the entire continent of Europe. From the Baltic, south, those barriers cut across Germany in a gash of barbed wire, concrete, dog runs, and guard towers. Farther south, there may be no visible, no obvious wall. But there remain armed guards and checkpoints all the same—still a restriction on the right to travel, still an instrument to impose

[1] A 7,500-acre forest located on the western side of Berlin.

[2] A large public park in the center of Berlin.

[3] Paul Lincke (1866–1946) was a German operetta composer. His "Das macht die Berliner Luft" ("This Makes the Berlin Air," 1904) is a beloved song about Berlin.

[4] "I still have a suitcase in Berlin." From Paul Lincke's song, "Das macht die Berliner Luft."

[5] There is only one Berlin.

upon ordinary men and women the will of a totalitarian state. Yet it is here in Berlin where the wall emerges most clearly; here, cutting across your city, where the news photo and the television screen have imprinted this brutal division of a continent upon the mind of the world. Standing before the Brandenburg Gate, every man is a German, separated from his fellow men. Every man is a Berliner, forced to look upon a scar.

President von Weizsäcker[6] has said: "The German question is open as long as the Brandenburg Gate is closed." Today I say: As long as this gate is closed, as long as this scar of a wall is permitted to stand, it is not the German question alone that remains open, but the question of freedom for all mankind. Yet I do not come here to lament. For I find in Berlin a message of hope, even in the shadow of this wall, a message of triumph.

In this season of spring in 1945, the people of Berlin emerged from their air raid shelters to find devastation. Thousands of miles away, the people of the United States reached out to help. And in 1947, Secretary of State—as you've been told—George Marshall announced the creation of what would become known as the Marshall Plan.[7] Speaking precisely 40 years ago this month, he said, "Our policy is directed not against any country or doctrine, but against hunger, poverty, desperation, and chaos."

In the Reichstag a few moments ago, I saw a display commemorating this 40th anniversary of the Marshall Plan. I was struck by the sign on a burnt-out, gutted structure that was being rebuilt. I understand that Berliners of my own generation can remember seeing signs like it dotted throughout the western sectors of the city. The sign read simply: "The Marshall Plan is helping here to strengthen the free world." A strong, free world in the West: That dream became real. Japan rose from ruin to become an economic giant. Italy, France, Belgium—virtually every nation in Western Europe saw political and economic rebirth; the European Community was founded.

In West Germany and here in Berlin, there took place an economic miracle,

[6] Richard von Weizsäcker (b. April 1920) was governing mayor of West Berlin from 1981 until 1984, president of West Germany from 1984 until 1990, and president of Germany from 1990 until 1994. He attended the ceremony.

[7] The Marshall Plan, officially called the European Recovery Program (1948-51) was the primary U.S. program for rebuilding the economic foundation of Western Europe in order to repel the threat of internal communism after World War II.

the *Wirtschaftswunder.*[8] Adenauer,[9] Erhard,[10] Reuter,[11] and other leaders understood the practical importance of liberty—that just as truth can flourish only when the journalist is given freedom of speech, so prosperity can come about only when the farmer and businessman enjoy economic freedom. The German leaders reduced tariffs, expanded free trade, lowered taxes. From 1950 to 1960 alone, the standard of living in West Germany and Berlin doubled.

> From devastation, from utter ruin, you Berliners have, in freedom, rebuilt a city that once again ranks as one of the greatest on earth.

Where four decades ago there was rubble, today in West Berlin there is the greatest industrial output of any city in Germany—busy office blocks, fine homes and apartments, proud avenues, and the spreading lawns of parkland. Where a city's culture seemed to have been destroyed, today there are two great universities, orchestras and an opera, countless theaters and museums. Where there was want, today there's abundance—food, clothing, automobiles—the wonderful goods of the Ku'damm.[12] From devastation, from utter ruin, you Berliners have, in freedom, rebuilt a city that once again ranks as one of the greatest on earth. The Soviets may have had other plans. But, my friends, there were a few things the Soviets didn't count on: *Berliner herz, Berliner humor, ja, und Berliner schnauze.*[13]

In the 1950s, Khrushchev predicted, "We will bury you."[14] But in the West

---

8 Literally, "economic miracle."

9 Konrad Adenauer (1876–1967) was chancellor of Germany from 1949 until 1963.

10 Ludwig Erhard (1897–1977) was chancellor of West Germany from 1963 until 1966.

11 Ernst Reuter (1889–1953) was mayor of Berlin from 1948 until 1953.

12 The Kurfürstendamm, known locally as the Ku'damm, is a long, broad boulevard of shops, houses, hotels, and restaurants. Many fashion designers and car manufacturers have showrooms there.

13 Literally, "Berliner heart, Berliner humor, yes, and Berliner mouth," but Berliner schnauze is also an expression that means "Berlin bluntness."

14 Nikita Khrushchev (1894–1971), Soviet premier from 1953 until 1964, famously used an expression generally translated into English as "We will bury you!" while addressing Western ambassadors at a reception at the Polish embassy in Moscow on November 18, 1956.

today, we see a free world that has achieved a level of prosperity and well-being unprecedented in all human history. In the Communist world we see failure, technological backwardness, declining standards of health, even want of the most basic kind—too little food. Even today, the Soviet Union still cannot feed itself. After these four decades, then, there stands before the entire world one great and inescapable conclusion: Freedom leads to prosperity. Freedom replaces the ancient hatreds among the nations with comity and peace. Freedom is the victor.

And now the Soviets themselves may, in a limited way, be coming to understand the importance of freedom. We hear much from Moscow about a new policy of reform and openness. Some political prisoners have been released. Certain foreign news broadcasts are no longer being jammed. Some economic enterprises have been permitted to operate with greater freedom from state control. Are these the beginnings of profound changes in the Soviet state? Or are they token gestures, intended to raise false hopes in the West or to strengthen the Soviet system without changing it? We welcome change and openness, for we believe that freedom and security go together, that the advance of human liberty can only strengthen the cause of world peace.

There is one sign the Soviets can make that would be unmistakable, that would advance dramatically the cause of freedom and peace. General Secretary Gorbachev, if you seek peace, if you seek prosperity for the Soviet Union and Eastern Europe, if you seek liberalization: Come here to this gate! Mr. Gorbachev, open this gate! Mr. Gorbachev, tear down this wall!

I understand the fear of war and the pain of division that afflict this continent—and I pledge to you my country's efforts to help overcome these burdens. To be sure, we in the West must resist Soviet expansion. So we must maintain defenses of unassailable strength. Yet we seek peace, so we must strive to reduce arms on both sides. Beginning 10 years ago, the Soviets challenged the Western alliance with a grave new threat, hundreds of new and more deadly SS-20 nuclear missiles, capable of striking every capital in Europe. The Western alliance responded by committing itself to a counterdeployment unless the Soviets agreed to negotiate a

> Come here to this gate! Mr. Gorbachev, open this gate! Mr. Gorbachev, tear down this wall!

better solution: namely, the elimination of such weapons on both sides. For many months, the Soviets refused to bargain in earnestness. As the alliance, in turn, prepared to go forward with its counterdeployment, there were difficult days—days of protests like those during my 1982 visit to this city—and the Soviets later walked away from the table.

> East and West do not mistrust each other because we are armed; we are armed because we mistrust each other.

But through it all, the alliance held firm. And I invite those who protested then—I invite those who protest today—to mark this fact: Because we remained strong, the Soviets came back to the table. And because we remained strong, today we have within reach the possibility, not merely of limiting the growth of arms, but of eliminating, for the first time, an entire class of nuclear weapons from the face of the earth. As I speak, NATO ministers are meeting in Iceland to review the progress of our proposals for eliminating these weapons. At the talks in Geneva, we have also proposed deep cuts in strategic offensive weapons. And the Western allies have likewise made far-reaching proposals to reduce the danger of conventional war and to place a total ban on chemical weapons.

While we pursue these arms reductions, I pledge to you that we will maintain the capacity to deter Soviet aggression at any level at which it might occur. And in cooperation with many of our allies, the United States is pursuing the Strategic Defense Initiative[15]—research to base deterrence not on the threat of offensive retaliation, but on defenses that truly defend; on systems, in short, that will not target populations but shield them. By these means we seek to increase the safety of Europe and all the world. But we must remember a crucial fact: East and West do not mistrust each other because we are armed; we are armed because we mistrust each other. And our differences are not about weapons but about liberty. When President Kennedy spoke at the city hall those 24 years ago, freedom was encircled. Berlin was under siege. And today, despite all the pressures upon this city, Berlin stands secure in its liberty. And freedom itself is transforming the globe.

In the Philippines, in South and Central America, democracy has been given

[15] Often popularly referred to as "Star Wars."

a rebirth. Throughout the Pacific, free markets are working miracle after miracle of economic growth. In the industrialized nations, a technological revolution is taking place—a revolution marked by rapid, dramatic advances in computers and telecommunications.

In Europe, only one nation and those it controls refuse to join the community of freedom. Yet in this age of redoubled economic growth, of information and innovation, the Soviet Union faces a choice: It must make fundamental changes, or it will become obsolete. Today thus represents a moment of hope. We in the West stand ready to cooperate with the East to promote true openness, to break down barriers that separate people, to create a safer, freer world.

And surely there is no better place than Berlin, the meeting place of East and West, to make a start. Free people of Berlin: Today, as in the past, the United States stands for the strict observance and full implementation of all parts of the Four Power Agreement of 1971. Let us use this occasion, the 750th anniversary of this city, to usher in a new era, to seek a still fuller, richer life for the Berlin of the future. Together, let us maintain and develop the ties between the Federal Republic and the western sectors of Berlin, which is permitted by the 1971 agreement.[16]

And I invite Mr. Gorbachev: Let us work to bring the eastern and western parts of the city closer together, so that all the inhabitants of all Berlin can enjoy the benefits that come with life in one of the great cities of the world. To open Berlin still further to all Europe, East and West, let us expand the vital air access to this city, finding ways of making commercial air service to Berlin more convenient, more comfortable, and more economical. We look to the day when West Berlin can become one of the chief aviation hubs in all central Europe.

With our French and British partners, the United States is prepared to help

> In this age of redoubled economic growth, information, and innovation, the Soviet Union faces a choice: It must make fundamental changes, or it will become obsolete.

---

[16] This agreement helped regularize trade and improve travel and communications between West Berlin and West Germany and, to a lesser degree, between East and West Berlin.

bring international meetings to Berlin. It would be only fitting for Berlin to serve as the site of United Nations meetings, or world conferences on human rights and arms control or other issues that call for international cooperation. There is no better way to establish hope for the future than to enlighten young minds,

The totalitarian world produces backwardness because it does such violence to the spirit, thwarting the human impulse to create, to enjoy, to worship.

and we would be honored to sponsor summer youth exchanges, cultural events, and other programs for young Berliners from the East. Our French and British friends, I'm certain, will do the same. And it's my hope that an authority can be found in East Berlin to sponsor visits from young people of the western sectors.

One final proposal, one close to my heart: Sport represents a source of enjoyment and ennoblement, and you may have noted that the Republic of Korea—South Korea—has offered to permit certain events of the 1988 Olympics to take place in the North. International sports competitions of all kinds could take place in both parts of this city. And what better way to demonstrate to the world the openness of this city than to offer in some future year to hold the Olympic Games here in Berlin, East and West?

In these four decades, as I have said, you Berliners have built a great city. You've done so in spite of threats—the Soviet attempts to impose the East Mark,[17] the blockade. Today the city thrives in spite of the challenges implicit in the very presence of this wall. What keeps you here? Certainly there's a great deal to be said for your fortitude, for your defiant courage. But I believe there's something deeper, something that involves Berlin's whole look and feel and way of life—not mere sentiment. No one could live long in Berlin without being completely disabused of illusions. Something, instead, that has seen the difficulties of life in Berlin but chose to accept them, that continues to build this good and proud city in contrast to a surrounding totalitarian presence that refuses to release human energies or

---

[17] On March 20, 1949, the occupying Western powers declared the West Mark the exclusive legal currency in the western sectors of Berlin. Still uncertain about the commitment of the Western powers to their city, many Berliners took heart from this linking of the economy of West Berlin with that of West Germany. See D. M. Giangreco and Robert E. Griffin, *Airbridge to Berlin: The Berlin Crisis of 1948, Its Origins and Aftermath* (Presidio Press, 1988).

aspirations. Something that speaks with a powerful voice of affirmation, that says yes to this city, yes to the future, yes to freedom. In a word, I would submit that what keeps you in Berlin is love—love both profound and abiding.

Perhaps this gets to the root of the matter, to the most fundamental distinction of all between East and West. The totalitarian world produces backwardness because it does such violence to the spirit, thwarting the human impulse to create, to enjoy, to worship. The totalitarian world finds even symbols of love and of worship an affront. Years ago, before the East Germans began rebuilding their churches, they erected a secular structure: the television tower at Alexanderplatz.[18] Virtually ever since, the authorities have been working to correct what they view as the tower's one major flaw, treating the glass sphere at the top with paints and chemicals of every kind. Yet even today, when the sun strikes that sphere—that sphere that towers over all Berlin—the light makes the sign of the cross. There in Berlin, like the city itself, symbols of love, symbols of worship, cannot be suppressed.

> This wall will fall. For it cannot withstand faith; it cannot withstand truth. The wall cannot withstand freedom.

As I looked out a moment ago from the Reichstag,[19] that embodiment of German unity, I noticed words crudely spray-painted upon the wall, perhaps by a young Berliner: "This wall will fall. Beliefs become reality." Yes, across Europe, this wall will fall. For it cannot withstand faith; it cannot withstand truth. The wall cannot withstand freedom.

And I would like, before I close, to say one word. I have read, and I have been questioned since I've been here, about certain demonstrations against my coming. And I would like to say just one thing, and to those who demonstrate so: I wonder if they have ever asked themselves that if they should have the kind of government they apparently seek, no one would ever be able to do what they're doing again.

Thank you and God bless you all.

---

[18] A large public square and transportation hub in central Berlin.

[19] The Reichstag building was constructed between 1884 and 1894 as the home of the parliament of the German Empire. It housed the Reichstag until 1933, when it was severely damaged in a fire. After World War II, it fell into disuse and was not fully restored until after German reunification in 1990. After its completion in 1999, it became the meeting place of the Bundestag, the modern German parliament.

I call upon... those who gave us nuclear weapons...to give us the means of rendering those nuclear weapons impotent and obsolete.

—ADDRESS ON DEFENSE AND NATIONAL SECURITY, MARCH 23, 1983

◀ **STAR WARS:** At the Martin Marietta Astronautics facility in Waterton, Colorado, November 24, 1987. "The Soviets may have overestimated our technical capacity," former secretary of state Henry Kissinger would later say. "On the other hand, we didn't have to build a complete version of SDI [the Strategic Defense Initiative] to make their calculations difficult. If the Soviets no longer knew how many missiles would get through, then they might have had to launch hundreds more to have had a chance of success." Yet the Soviets could never have afforded hundreds more. "You can see," said Kissinger, "why SDI had them rattled."

▲ **TIME CHECK:** In the Diplomatic Reception Room on December 9, 1987, the second day of their Washington summit. Sharing a light moment, Reagan and Gorbachev check their watches while waiting for their wives. "Well, at last it's over," Reagan would write in his diary that evening. "They've departed and I think the whole thing was the best summit we've ever had with the Soviet Union."

◄ **ARMS CONTROL:** In the Oval Office on December 8, 1987, the president and the general secretary hold the first meeting of the Washington summit. Six years earlier, when Reagan announced the "zero option," which called for the elimination of all intermediate-range nuclear weapons on both sides, the Soviets angrily broke off negotiations. A few hours after this photograph was taken, Reagan and Gorbachev would sit next to one another at a table in the East Room to sign the INF Treaty, which mandated the elimination of all intermediate-range nuclear weapons, almost exactly as Reagan had originally proposed. The Cold War was drawing to a close.

▲ **STREETS OF MOSCOW:** Waving to Russians during the third day of the Moscow summit, May 31, 1988. Reagan had just addressed students at Moscow State University. "Freedom," he said, "is the right to question...the established way of doing things. It is the continuing revolution of the marketplace...[It] is the recognition that...no single authority of government has a monopoly on the truth, but that every individual life is infinitely precious." The 40th president, describing freedom to the children of the Soviet apparat—a sure sign that the Cold War was over.

▶ **RED SQUARE:** The president and the first lady in Red Square, gazing toward St. Basil's Cathedral, June 1, 1988. The Reagans had just returned from dinner at the home of the Gorbachevs. "On the way back," the president explained in his diary, "we drove through Red Square so Nancy could see it...Believe it [or] not there were hundreds of people behind a rope there to see & wave at us...It was almost midnight."

Whatever else
history may say
about me when
I'm gone, I hope
it will record that
I appealed to
your best hopes,
not your worst
fears; to your
confidence rather
than your doubts.

—LAST PUBLIC SPEECH, REPUBLICAN
CONVENTION, AUGUST 17, 1992

▶ **SUCCESSOR:** President Reagan and
Vice President Bush on the terrace outside the Oval Office, July 7, 1988. Opponents during the GOP presidential contest eight years earlier, Reagan and Bush
became close friends. This photograph
was taken on a Thursday, the day each
week when the two men lunched together, exchanging their thoughts in private.

◄◄ **OPENING NIGHT (PREVIOUS PAGES):** The Republican National Convention at the New Orleans Superdome, August 15, 1988. "When people tell me that I became president on January 20th, 1981," Reagan, now just months from leaving office, told the convention, "I feel I have to correct them. You don't become president of the United States. You are given temporary custody of an institution called the presidency, which belongs to our people." Three days later, Vice President Bush would accept his party's nomination to succeed President Reagan.

◄ **PRESS BOX:** Wrigley Field, September 30, 1988. As the Chicago Cubs play the Pittsburgh Pirates—the game would go 10 innings, with the Pirates defeating the Cubs 10 to 9—Ronald Reagan, who began his career broadcasting Cubs games just over half a century earlier, swaps stories with the legendary baseball announcer Harry Caray.

It was his goal and his dream to end his term and enter history as a peacemaker.

—Mikhail Gorbachev,
June 6, 2004

▶ **HAND-OVER:** President Reagan, President-elect Bush, and General Secretary Gorbachev meet on Governors Island in New York Harbor, December 7, 1988. This was the fifth and final Reagan-Gorbachev summit meeting. Addressing the United Nations earlier that day, Gorbachev announced that the Soviet Union would soon make sharp reductions in its military establishment. "I think the meeting was a tremendous success," Reagan wrote in his diary that evening. "A better attitude than at any of our previous meetings... [Gorbachev] sounded as if he saw us as partners making a better world."

◄ **GIPPER'S SWEATER:** In the Rose Garden, January 18, 1989. Two days before leaving office, President Reagan hosts the Notre Dame football team, which won the 1988 NCAA national football championship. The Reverend Edward Malloy, president of Notre Dame, presents Reagan with a sweater that belonged to the legendary Notre Dame football star George Gipp, a.k.a. "the Gipper." Reagan came to be known by the same nickname after portraying Gipp in the 1940 film *Knute Rockne, All American.*

▲ **FINAL DAY:** The 40th president of the United States leaves the Oval Office for the last time, January 20, 1989, 9:58 a.m. "A little before 10 AM I went over to the Oval O.," Reagan would write in his diary that evening. "[It was] looking pretty bare." In eight years Reagan had survived an assassination attempt, revived the economy, restored the nation's morale, and, as Prime Minister Margaret Thatcher would later put it, "won the Cold War without firing a shot."

Photograph by Pete Souza

▲ HEADING HOME: Aboard Marine One, January 20, 1989. After attending the inauguration of President George Bush at the Capitol, the former president and the first lady boarded the presidential helicopter for the flight to Andrews Air Force Base, where Air Force One was waiting to carry them home to California. The most powerful man in the world only a few minutes before, private citizen Reagan waves farewell to Washington.

▶▶ AT PEACE (FOLLOWING PAGES): President Reagan riding his favorite mount, El Alamein, at Rancho del Cielo in 1986. Freebo and Victory trot along behind. After leaving office, Reagan spent as much time at the ranch as he could, making the trip from Los Angeles most weekends. When Alzheimer's disease finally made it unsafe for Reagan to ride, Mrs. Reagan asked John Barletta, a Secret Service agent assigned to the ranch, to break the news to the former chief executive. Barletta struggled, choking back tears. "And he got up," Barletta would later say. "And he put his hands on my shoulders. And he said, 'It's okay, John. I know.'"

LETTER TO THE AMERICAN PEOPLE

November 5, 1994

My Fellow Americans,

I have recently been told that I am one of the Americans who will be afflicted with Alzheimer's Disease.

Upon learning this news, Nancy & I had to decide whether as private citizens we would keep this a private matter or whether we would make this news known in a public way.

In the past Nancy suffered from breast cancer and I had my cancer surgeries. We found through our open disclosures we were able to raise public awareness. We were happy that as a result many more people underwent testing. They were treated in early stages and able to return to normal, healthy lives.

So now, we feel it is important to share it with you. In opening our hearts, we hope this might promote greater awareness of this condition. Perhaps it will encourage a clearer understanding of the individuals and families who are affected by it.

At the moment I feel just fine. I intend to live the remainder of the years God gives me on this earth doing the things I have always done. I will continue to share life's journey with my beloved Nancy and my family. I plan to enjoy the great outdoors and stay in touch with my friends and supporters.

Unfortunately, as Alzheimer's Disease progresses, the family often bears a heavy burden. I only wish there was some way I could spare Nancy from this painful experience. When the time comes I am confident that with your help she will face it with faith and courage.

In closing let me thank you, the American people, for giving me the great honor of allowing me to serve as your President. When the Lord calls me home, whenever that may be, I will face it with the greatest love for this country of ours and eternal optimism for its future.

I now begin the journey that will lead me into the sunset of my life. I know that for America there will always be a bright dawn ahead.

Thank you, my friends. May God always bless you.

▲ **LAST GOOD-BYE:** Mrs. Reagan lays her hand on the casket of her husband as he lies in state in the Capitol Rotunda, June 9, 2004. She had cared for the former president during the final decade of life, eventually becoming the only person he still recognized. Reagan died at their home in Bel Air, California, on June 5. He was 93. His casket rests on the same catafalque used at the funeral of Abraham Lincoln.

▶ **LYING IN STATE:** Photographed from the Capitol Dome, June 10, 2004. "We have lost a great president, a great American, and a great man," former prime minister Margaret Thatcher said during the funeral at the National Cathedral the following day. "Others hoped, at best, for an uneasy cohabitation with the Soviet Union... [Ronald Reagan] won the Cold War—not only without firing a shot, but also by inviting enemies out of their fortress and turning them into friends... And so today the world—in Prague, in Budapest, in Warsaw, in Sofia, in Bucharest, in Kiev, and in Moscow itself—the world mourns the passing of the Great Liberator and echoes his prayer, 'God Bless America.'"

Photographs by David Hume Kennerly

▶▶ **FINAL RESTING PLACE (FOLLOWING PAGES):** At the Reagan Library in Simi Valley, California. The gravesite looks out over rolling hills to the Pacific.

Contributors

Created by David Elliot Cohen

Text by Peter Robinson

Foreword by Newt Gingrich and Callista Gingrich

Designed by Peter Truskier and David Elliot Cohen

Page production and image processing by Peter Truskier, Premedia Systems, Inc.

Copyedited by Sherri Schultz

Proofread by Karen Parkin

Photography Credits

Contact Press Images: pages 2–3

Warner Bros. publicity photo: page 22

Hulton Archive/Getty Images: pages 23, 24

Getty Images: pages 214, 220, 221

All other photographs appear courtesy of the Ronald Reagan Presidential Library

Special Thanks

The Ronald Reagan Presidential Library

Steve Branch and Michael Pinckney of the National Archives and Records Administration

Michael Fragnito, Barbara Berger, and Fred Pagan of Sterling Publishing

Bill and Laurie Grayson

John Hammergren

Nicole Reed and Diane Ellis of the Hoover Institution, Stanford University

References

The story about "Moon" Reagan on page 8 is from Diane Bell, *The San Diego Union Tribune*, June 12, 2004.

The Reagan quotations on pages 29, 83, and 169 are from Lou Cannon, *President Reagan: The Role of a Lifetime* (Public Affairs, 2000).

The quotations on pages 34 and 45 are from *I Love You, Ronnie: The Letters of Ronald Reagan to Nancy Reagan*, edited by Nancy Reagan (Random House, 2002).

The Reagan quotations on pages 5, 11, 13, 14, 16, 27, 31, 63, 111, and 141 are from Ronald Reagan, *An American Life* (Simon & Schuster, 1990).

Excerpts from Ronald Reagan's diaries on pages 89, 94, 98, 108, 134, 139, 163, 169, 175, 184, 201, 202, 210, and 214 are from Ronald Reagan, *The Reagan Diaries Unabridged*, vols. 1 and 2), edited by Douglas Brinkley (Harper, 2009).

Speeches and excerpts from speeches delivered by Ronald Reagan during his presidency are from The Ronald Reagan Presidential Library, *The Public Papers of the President: Ronald Reagan, 1981 - 1989*.

The quotations on pages 37, 42, 67, 104, 107, 141, 184, 199, and 215 represent original research by the writer of this book. Some previously appeared in Peter Robinson, *How Ronald Reagan Changed My Life* (Harper, 2003).